WORDS OF LOVE 1959-2009 by Gary Clevenger © Copyright 2010

No Part of This Publication May Be Copied or Reproduced Without the Written Consent of the Editor / Author Gary Clevenger on <u>icon9736@hotmail.com</u>

Compiled and Edited By Gary Clevenger

UK Edition Edited By Peter Gibson and Tony Warran

Front Cover Collage by Don Larson

Front Cover & Back Cover Layouts by Scott Sriver

Editor's Note

I was born in 1959 in Lansing Michigan and grew up in Elkhart Indiana. My family would eventually move to South Bend Indiana in the 1970s where I still live today. I am a warehouse worker married for twenty years and have three kids and ten grandkids. My entire family realized long ago my love for the music that those three entertainers left us, and often refer to me as 'The Worlds Biggest Buddy Holly fan', but then again I must realize that's a title that most of us share

As I got into my teenage years I discovered the music and the magic of Buddy Holly while on a summer vacation at my Aunt and Uncle's house in Riverdale Michigan. I was eleven years old. I became very aware of the different types of music streaming out of the radio and television, and that my friends listened to. Rock 'n' roll music from the 1950s became an important part of my listening pleasure, and one song in particular created a lasting impression on me – 'That'll be the day'.

I actually discovered the music and magic of Buddy Holly by listening to the album 'The Buddy Holly Story' on Coral Records. The song that affected me the most was 'Peggy Sue Got Married'. It was a powerful song and so different, some how. So, I found Buddy Holly. Then there was Ritchie with his rough and raucous rocker, 'Come on Let's Go", and the Bopper with his teasing and joyful 'Chantilly Lace'.

The event that took place on February 3, 1959, was a great tragedy and four young lives were lost that night, including the pilot of the plane – Roger Peterson, who must be included, and is sometimes forgotten when talking about 'The Day the Music Died'. We must remember on that day four lives were lost and that four families grieved at the loss of their family member.

Back in 2007 I was thinking back to what happened, and how I had first heard the magic and timeless music played by those wonderful guys. I then wondered how other fans had discovered their music. So, the idea for a book with contributions from the fans was born. I posted messages on websites and before long I was receiving stories from all over the world about how people had found and enjoyed, and could never forget, the music. I was given help, especially by Vicky and John Pickering, to contact people who knew Buddy at Lubbock High School.

I was blessed to have talked to many of Buddy's classmates at Lubbock High (Class of 55). They shared many exciting and interesting stories about growing up in Lubbock, Texas and of course stories about their friend and fellow classmate Charles Hardin Holley.
I have to thank many people for their help, and I hope they are all named in the list at the end of the book. It has been a long road, and a hard struggle at times, to get here, but I think it has been worth it. I sincerely hope you agree and that you enjoy reading this book!

Gary Clevenger

DEDICATED TO

THE FAMILY and FRIENDS of

BUDDY HOLLY

RITCHIE VALENS

THE BIG BOPPER

ROGER PETERSON

Bob Hale at The Surf Ballroom
With Carroll Anderson
1st Anniversary of KRIB
Rock 'n' Roll format
1959

Buddy's Last Night – Ritchie's, Bopper's and Roger's, Also!

By: Bob Hale

On February 2nd 1959 the bus carrying Frankie Sardo, Dion and the Belmonts, Buddy and the (Road Show) Crickets, Big Bopper (J.P. Richardson), and Ritchie Valens drove into Clear Lake, Iowa – finally! The bus was late. The bus was cold; smelled of weeks of dirty laundry; and, it was a lousy-riding bus to begin with.

Buddy Holly came off the bus, along with road manager Sam Geller, tired, sore, and upset and in a hurry. He needed to set up, rehearse, and to eat. Eat! They all were hungry. Some ate at the Surf Ballroom's small restaurant; some found a couple of local spots open. And they ate in a hurry. They needed to get the stage set and become used to the Surf's sound system – one microphone! That's it – one mic!

While Buddy noodled on the piano, Sam Geller took me aside and said that I was looking at a future "genius, a leader, and one of the biggest names to rise in show business." Geller, one who knew dozens of musicians, and who had worked with all the biggest names, considered Buddy Holly to be the best of the best of the young new talent.
"You watch him; in 5 or 10 years, Holly will be one of the biggest and wealthiest performers in show business. He is a genius, and one of the nicest persons I've ever met."

Geller had nothing but kind words to spread around all of the performers. "You'll never hear a naughty word or dirty joke from any one of them!"
That was the group about to perform for nearly 1800 teens that night. It was the largest teen crowd the Surf had ever experienced. It was also one of the biggest in the ballroom's history, up to that point, according to Carroll Anderson, ballroom manager.

During the intermission we set up for Dion and the Belmonts and Holly. The first half featured Frankie Sardo, well received for a young man who was trying to break into show business; Ritchie Valens, who rocked the place and had the girls nearly swooning.

(Contrary to the popular musical 'Buddy', Ritchie was not a hip-swinging teen on the prowl, eager to get to his hot lady in Fargo! Valens had never been to North Dakota; he'd never been west!) This was his first tour. It was also his first taste of bitter winter weather. It's too bad that he is depicted as something far less than he was – a classy, shy, young man on the way to super stardom. Valens had become one of the first Latinos to break into the top of the musical charts. He was destined to be a super-star!

Big Bopper – J.P. Richardson - was home-sick. His wife was expecting, and when he sat next to my wife, Kathy, also expecting, he asked if he could feel the little one move.

"That's what I miss so much – being home so I can feel my baby growing!" That recollection brought many tears the next morning.

Because the regular drummer, Charlie Bunch was left behind in a Green Bay hospital with frost-bitten feet (Oh, that bus was cold!) Buddy filled in during the Belmonts' segment. When they wrapped it up I sat with Dion on the riser in front of the drum set. I asked him to introduce his band, and when he came to the drummer he explained that Bunch had been left behind.

"So, we hire this new guy...sort of young, but not too bad. He also sings. His name is...um, who...oh yeah, Buddy Holly!"

With that Buddy jumped up from the drums, grabbed his guitar, and band members switched places. As they did, Buddy broke into "Gotta Travel On," backing himself up with his guitar while the band members switched places.

I reported to some two dozen radio stations the next day; about 10 newspapers and wire services also called. It was an event that linked me with one of the greatest tragedies to hit the American entertainment scene. And, today I am always asked: "Where would they be today?"

Still making people smile; still making their feet tap; still making them dance. Fifty years later, they are greatly missed!

Bob Hale, Winter Dance Party emcee 1959 - Clear Lake, Iowa.

What hits me every time I walk out there is the timelessness of the music.

The '50s and early '60s turned out music that has staying power - it's as danceable today as the day it was recorded. And, the tunes and lyrics are memorable - something that is lacking in so much of today's music.

And that music was something you could sing along with - everyone learned the lyrics and they have become, in many cases, part of our culture. Like Bing Crosby's "White Christmas," a lot of the Top 40 hits remain with us. Crosby, Cole and Como were not the only ones, however to make permanent marks on our culture. The list is endless because the music of the '50s was broad in scope - from hard rock and roll to gentle cha-cha. Jerry Lee Lewis to Ben E. King, from Elvis to the Everly Brothers; from Buddy Holly to Little Richard... the comparisons could go on all day!

Many of the hit-makers of the 50s - Holly and Elvis come to mind - were "at home" in many moods. Love ballads to hard rock. My Elvis collection has every beat imaginable. The Holly lists show a talent who was equally comfortable across the spectrum.

We are now a half century removed from the music of the '50s, yet that music is as danceable, as listenable, and memorable as it was "way back then." Put on a Ben E. King record and feet begin to tap...and people get up and dance!

What passes for popular music today will not be remembered in 25, 20, 10 even 5 years from now - and that's OK, because so much that is written today is not intended to have staying power. It's acknowledged to be "passing" so we can't expect to hit the dance floor 10 years from now to one of today's top sellers.

Bob Hale - 2009

I MISS YOU RITCHIE EVERYDAY
I MISS YOUR MUSIC IN EVERY WAY
I PLAY YOUR RECORDS ON MY GUITAR
THEY DONT SOUND THE SAME WAY THAT THEY WERE

I WISH I COULD HAVE SEEN YOU ON STAGE
THE WAY YOU HELD AN AUDIENCE AT SUCH A YOUNG AGE
THAT'S MY LITTLE SUZIE, IN A TURKISH TOWN
I LOVE YOUR MUSIC MAN WHAT A SOUND

EVERYWHERE YOU GO PEOPLE KNOW WHO YOU ARE
DONNA, LA BAMBA THAT'S WHAT MADE YOU A STAR
IT WENT TO THE TOP WAS A NUMBER ONE
RITCHIE I MISS YOU SO DOES EVERYONE

WHY WERE YOU TAKEN AT SUCH A YOUNG AGE
YOU HAD THE TALENT MAN TO SING ON A STAGE
I OFTEN WONDER WHAT YOU'RE DOING NOW
SINGING OR PLAYING YOUR GUITAR ON A CLOUD

RITCHIE I MISS YOU, SO DOES EVERYONE

LYRICS BY JASON SEYMOUR
© COPYRIGHT 2008

On stage at Fournier's Ballroom, Eau Claire, Wisconsin - January 26, 1959

My Winter Dance Party Story
January 26, 1959

I was lucky enough to be there, so here is my story.

Fourniers (fur-knee-ers) Ballroom: the Winter Dance Party had come to town. It was a Monday night, January 26, 1959. It was a school night and I was 17 years old and a senior in high school.

My prime reason for going was to see Buddy Holly; he was the one I admired. I had the Chirping Crickets album and almost all of the 45's. I went to the Meyer Music Store a few weeks before the concert and bought my ticket for only $1.00 (rather than paying $1.25 at the door)! The tickets were just like a fair ride ticket, unlike nowadays, with the date, names of the performers, venue, etc.

I went to the show with a friend of mine, Glen St. Arnault. He picked me up in his Dad's car and we drove down to Fournier's about 3 miles away. It was really cold that night. The temperature was -2, back then they didn't factor in the wind chill: if they had, it would have been closer to -20.

We checked our coats and headed for the bandstand to get a good place to stand. Concerts back then were different than now. They were dances and you danced or you stood and watched. I chose the latter because I was afraid of girls back then. Also, I didn't want to be anywhere but close to the bandstand. The show started off with Frankie Sardo; however, I can't remember that much about him. I do remember thinking that he couldn't carry a tune in a bag. After him came Dion and the Belmont's and then The Big Bopper. I did like them and they sang most of their hit records. The Bopper was a really crazy guy, performing lot of antics on stage. He was followed by teenager Ritchie Valens. I recall him singing La Bamba and Donna. Each act performed about seven songs; that was a lot back in those days. Another interesting thing is that the same backup band was up there all night long.

I couldn't wait till Buddy and the Crickets. All of a sudden there he was I was standing only about five feet away from him. But wait a minute: the backup band was still up there. Where were the Crickets? These guys didn't look like any of the guys on the cover of the Chirping Crickets album cover. These weren't the Crickets - but that was Buddy Holly in the flesh and that was all I cared about. Little did I know at that time that I was looking at Tommy Allsup on guitar, Carl Bunch on drums, and, over on the left side playing bass guitar: Waylon Jennings.

Buddy sang seven songs: Gotta Travel On; Peggy Sue; That'll Be The Day; Heartbeat; Be Bop a Lula; Whole Lot of Shakin'; and It Doesn't Matter Anymore. He didn't talk much. He was wearing black shoes, gray slacks, a black blazer and a black shirt and a white silk dickey. To this day I don't know why I didn't go up and shake his hand or even ask for an autograph. Back in those days who would have thought of getting autographs?

Then, all too soon, the show was over and I went home a very happy guy because I had seen my hero, Buddy Holly. A week later on February 3, 1959, we all know what happened that day. It was one of the worst days of my life. I heard the news on the radio at high school that day. I just couldn't believe it, how could this have happened? I and the entire rock and roll world were in shock.

In 1961 I started dating a girl from Withee, Wisconsin about 40 some miles east of Eau Claire. She was going to school in Eau Claire for nurses training. One weekend I went home with her to meet her parents. While we were there she brought out a picture book and we looked at pictures of her aunts and uncles and cousins and such. I turned one of the pages and I couldn't believe my eyes. There on this page were pictures of Buddy, Ritchie, the Bopper and Sardo and one of the Belmont's. I asked her where she got these pictures and she said that she was there that night. Then she said, "I know what a Buddy Holly fan you are, would you like to have the pictures"? Well needless to say that I was thrilled to have them. I took them home and put them in a scrapbook and there they stayed until a day in 1976 when I found out about a book that someone had written about Buddy. But then that's another whole story.

Later on in my life, I met Waylon Jennings and was proud to be his friend for over 26 years. It was amazing to stand backstage during a Waylon concert and see and hear over 20,000 people screaming. It's something I know Buddy would have been a part of had fate not intervened. I also got to know the real Crickets and have been friends with them since 1978. I was honored to meet Buddy's Mom and Dad as well as his brothers and sister. When I met Dion, I showed him pictures from the Winter Dance Party and I made him copies of the pictures. I was invited by Columbia Pictures to the world premiere of the movie, The Buddy Holly Story. It was all because of the pictures my girlfriend gave me. I went to a class reunion some years ago and a class mate gave me 9 more pictures from that night. They had been stored in a scrapbook in her basement all these years. I was blown away when she presented them to me. It was like finding a buried treasure. So now I am the proud owner of 17 pictures from that night. The pictures have been in books and magazines all over the world.

In 1989, on a lark, a friend and I recreated the Winter Dance Party tour. We did sock hops in all 11 cities and traveled just like they did in 1959. We drove a total of 2,764 miles and played in five of the original ballrooms, the others having been either torn down, burned down, or used for something else. We played records, but never one that was recorded after February 2, 1959: only what Buddy and the rest would have heard.

So there you have my story. Just remember, the music didn't die, cause Buddy Holly Lives every time we play rock'n'roll !

Don Larson

On stage at Fournier's Ballroom, Eau Claire, Wisconsin - January 26, 1959

On stage at Fournier's Ballroom, Eau Claire, Wisconsin - January 26, 1959

SECOND HAND BOPPER MEMORIES

ONLY THINGS I KNOW ABOUT MY DAD COME FROM STORIES OTHER FOLKS HAVE TOLD OF COURSE. I HAVE ALL HIS MILLION SELLERS ON MY WALL COATED IN GOLD.

THRU THE YEARS PAST I'VE LEARNED TO LOVE A MAN I'LL NEVER KNOW OR SEE I JUST WISH I HAD SOMETHING MORE THAN SECOND HAND BOPPER MEMORIES.

I OFTEN WONDER WHAT INSPIRED HIM TO WRITE A SONG LIKE 'CHANTILLY LACE' WHEN I ASK MY MOM IF IT WAS HER SHE JUST SMILES AND GETS A FARAWAY LOOK ON HER FACE.

THERE'S NOT A NIGHT THAT PASSES THAT HE DOESN'T WALK THRU MY DREAMS AND HAVE A TALK WITH ME.

I JUST WISH I HAD SOMETHING MORE THAN SECOND HAND BOPPER MEMORIES.

I HAD A DREAM LONG AGO AND SOMEDAY I HOPE TO FOLLOW IT THRU TO TRAVEL AROUND THIS WORLD AND MEET ALL THE PEOPLE MY DADDY KNEW THEN MY HEART COULD BE AT REST, AND MY OLE MIND SET FREE.

I JUST WISH I HAD MORE THAN SECOND HAND BOPPER MEMORIES

JAY P RICHARDSON

I was just a little girl, but my Uncle Buddy Holly meant a lot to me. He used to carry me around and sing to me. Our church had a large basement and that is where the Sunday school kids would go. Back in those days, a lot of people went to church. It was quite crowded. I was always getting lost and couldn't find my parents. So my Uncle Buddy grabbed me by the hand and helped me to get to my parents.

My parents and I never missed Sunday night services at the church. But one particular Sunday we missed because Uncle Buddy was going to be on the Ed Sullivan show and we all wanted to see him perform. You couldn't record TV back in those days; so you had to see the real thing. We stayed home that night just to see Buddy perform. I will never forget it.

The Christmas before he was killed, he and Maria Elena gave me a beautiful lady doll. I still have it. I'll never part with it.

He was such an inspiration to me. I don't think I would have ever sung professionally or write songs, if he had not been such an inspiration.

Sherry Holley (2009)

Believe it or not, I fired Buddy and his group from the all-school talent show.

I was the student director, with the policy drilled into me by Mr. Howell, the speech and drama teacher, that if one didn't show up for rehearsal, one could not take part.

Sarah Simmons (class of '56) was in charge of the dance part of the program. This was to be modeled after "Your Hit Parade," a TV show of the current top musical hits. The square dancers would be coordinated with the live music provided by various students--solo singers and group singers. Buddy and his group didn't show for the first two rehearsals, so he was OUT Students must have intervened with the faculty sponsor (maybe Mrs. Bailey--I don't really remember), because she told me I should give the group another chance. Since this was 1955 and respect for adults was still in order, I called Buddy and told him that he was back on the program if he showed up for the last rehearsals. He did. As I watched from right backstage (the group was performing from right frontstage), I admitted to myself that, in the words of other students who begged me to put Buddy and his group back on the program, he really is good.

Margaret Condray (now Peggy Thomas)   2009

I was minus 17 years old in 1959 so it would take me close to 31 years to become a teenager myself and discover the "Big Beat" -- the rock and roll music of the 1950s.

I grew up in Montreal, Canada and in the early 90s (at around 15 years old) I was lucky enough to discover that an "Oldies" radio station had hit the airwaves here in the city. Well, that did it! My dial was set on Oldies 990 forever from that point on.

I was soon being introduced to hits by The Everly Brothers, Sam Cooke, The Beatles, Chuck Berry, The Platters, Elvis Presley, Dion, Buddy Holly, Ricky Nelson, Ritchie Valens, Jerry Lee Lewis, Fats Domino and on and on and on. I was absorbing all of it, studying the charts from that period, buying all those old records (on CD) and requesting songs daily to the point where they knew my name at the station. It wasn't long before I grew fascinated with Buddy Holly as every February 2nd and 3rd, they had tribute shows and spoke about Holly, Valens and J.P. and their last fateful tour.

But it was his music; it was all those great songs of his that really made an impression. From 'Everyday' to 'It Doesn't Matter Anymore' to 'Rave On', every time you hear a Buddy Holly song, it brings you back to an innocent time and place where the music was great and the artists who sang them were cooler than cool. Sure, the lyrics were simple but that doesn't make them connect to a lovesick teenager any less. In fact, it connects all the more because they came from a kid who was that age when he wrote them, and believed every word when he sang those lyrics.

A Buddy Holly fan in the great movie American Hot Wax said it best: "Buddy Holly Lives." As far as rock and roll deaths go, to me, the most tragic, the most heartbreaking one will always be the one that occurred on February 3rd, 1959. I have been attending the tribute shows in Clear Lake, IA since 2004. If you need to know the impression these 3 musicians made on the rock and roll world, look no further than the Surf Ballroom on February of every year. We celebrate their lives and their music and we let the guys up there in rock and roll heaven know that all they did in their all too short lives, will never be forgotten. The trio can look down to Clear Lake, IA, Buffalo, NY, London, England, Montreal, Canada and even Stockholm, Sweden and they will see always some young kid enjoying their music, 50 years later...

What are my thoughts about the musicians & the music? I can go on for hours but I won't because it can best be summed up by a lyric from the greatest song ever written and a little addition by me at the end.

"A long, long time ago, I can still remember how that music used to make me smile..."

Sevan Garabedian

BUDDY HOLLY NOT FADE AWAY

Verse 1:
Little Buddy Holly was born in '36.
Mom and Daddy wasn't poor,
but you sure couldn't call him rich.
Well, a white tee shirt and faded blue jeans -
Would that be the color of fame?
Very few people knew Charles Hardin was his name.

Verse 2:
He was born to sing; Buddy had a natural sound,
Like a bird on the wing or a cricket in a crack in the ground,
He could never go wrong with a simple love song,
And a beat like the Texas wind
Caught him in a whirl like a cyclone's swirl -
Brought him fame all over the world.

Chorus:
And he sang his way from a country boy
To a place among the stars.
That's where he sings and heaven rings
With rock and roll guitars.
And the soul that he is and the soul that he was
Never laid down 'neath the sod.
Momma raised him in the church;
And Buddy is at home with God.
Buddy Holly not fade away.

Verse 3:
Mason City and the snow was afallin' down.
Buddy ought not to fly - the plane shouldn't leave the ground.
But, time wouldn't wait, and he couldn't be late
To sing in another town.
Buddy, you're gonna go where there ain't no snow –
God's gonna call you home.

Last Chorus:
And he sang his way from a country boy
To a place among the stars.
That's where he sings and heaven rings
With rock and roll guitars.
And the soul that he is and the soul that he was
Never laid down `neath the sod.
Momma raised him in the church,
And Buddy is at home with God.
Buddy Holly not fade away.

Coda:
Singing "Peggy Sue", "True Love Ways",
and "When I Die, That'll Be The Day".
Singing "Words of Love", "Everyday".
Buddy Holly not fade away.

Music and Lyrics by
John W. Pickering
© 1986 John Pickering Music Co.

John Pickering's Memories of
Charles Hardin Holley through 1957 in Lubbock, Texas

My family knew the Holley family long before Buddy Holley was old enough to perform. When Buddy was age 4, I was 8 years old and in the second grade. My brother Bill was 14 years old and in the 9th grade at Carroll Thompson Junior High School at Lubbock, Texas. My family – The Pickering Family Quartet – was performing daily on Radio Station KFYO at Lubbock. The Holley family members were regular listeners to our show, and Travis Holley, Buddy's older brother, was a good friend of Billy Pickering, as he was called then. They "ran together" some then and in ensuing years.

My family (Mom, Pop, Billy and Johnny) would perform at gospel singing conventions throughout West Texas/Eastern New Mexico, and we performed gospel/secular concerts at school auditoriums most every weekend. During this time we became acquainted with members of the Holley family, especially older brothers Larry and Travis Holley, who played accordion and guitar and sang duets together. Their little brother Buddy was inspired at home by the singing and picking of his family members, including Buddy's mother Ella and his sister Pat, who would sing around the piano. L.O. Holley, Buddy's father, was a great lover of music and encouraged his family to sing and play. He was primarily an enabler and a Baptist who loved all kinds of music, especially gospel.

My wife, Vicky Billington, attended Lubbock High School with Buddy Holley and Jerry Allison and graduated with them in 1955. She went on to Texas Tech after graduation.

My cousin, Gerald "Jerry" Nixon attended school at nearby Roosevelt community, and he remembers Buddy and Bob Montgomery playing guitars and singing country songs on the bus from Lubbock and back from Roosevelt School. This was in the early 50s. Buddy and Bob were country boys and country singers/songwriters at a time when most Lubbock teenagers were pop music fans. Lubbock did not even have a full-time country radio station until Dave Stone opened KDAV in September 1953.

In 1952, my family, having been on a 50,000-watt Radio Station KTRH in Houston for about 4 years, moved back to Lubbock so that I could attend college at Texas Tech. We sang daily on Radio Station KSEL, and did a live concert every Saturday morning at Paramount Studio (one of our sponsors) where listeners could attend and buy TV sets. Our lead guitarist, Sonny Stewart was a good friend of Sonny Curtis and taught Curtis guitar licks in the style of Chet Atkins and Merle Travis. Sometimes Buddy Holley and members of his group would stop by our performances. After KDAV opened in 1953, at the request of Hi-Pockets Duncan, my family often sang on that station's Sunday Show, and Buddy Holley and Jack Neal soon began a regular country music program there, including both country and an occasional gospel song.

I was a Texas Tech student during this period of time, and Buddy Holley was in high school, I never ran around with high-schoolers except for Vicky Billington (who became my wife in 1957) and her friends.

I'd already met members of Buddy's musical groups at various times, especially Don Guess at Clovis in 1942 and Sonny Curtis in the early fifties. Both were fine musicians even when much younger, and both went on to solid musical careers in their own right.

In the mid-fifties I had a weekly radio show at KDAV Lubbock and at various times while there would see and hear Buddy Holley, Don Guess, Jack Neal, Sonny Curtis, Larry Welborn, and others . I met them all during this time. I sang on a weekend show featuring pianist Lawrence Ivey, and our music was very different from the country music of the above group.

Lawrence Ivey was an early member of the world-famous Stamps Quartet (1937), and in 1953 was the pianist for my versatile KFYO quartet called "The Plainsmen". Lawrence taught piano at a local music store, and I sang and served as master of ceremonies for songs that he taught his students. Therefore I was singing the hit pop songs of the time, which was in early 1954. Pop songs like "Secret Love" were a far-cry from the "Johnny and Jack"-type country music of Holley's group. But, my family prided itself on versatility and until my father's death in 1953, we sang all kinds of songs except hillbilly on our radio and concert shows.

But, I was in the audience at Lubbock high School when Buddy (Holley), Bob (Montgomery), and Larry (Welborn) switched from country music to Buddy's solos of Elvis-inspired rockabilly. This was before Jerry Allison and Joe B. Maudlin joined Buddy's group.

Thereafter, beginning in July, 1957, my relationship with Buddy Holly (his professional name) dealt with him as a professional. My brother Bill, Bob Lapham, and I backed him vocally on 9 of the first 12 "The Crickets" releases.

John Pickering "The Picks"

The Picks - John Pickering, Bob Lapham and Bill Pickering,
Petty Studio 1957
© John Pickering

The Buddy Holly Convention
August 26 - 27, 1978
Wethersfield, Connecticut

Maria Elena had the flu and couldn't come. Big disappointment. However, there were about 100 Holly fans there from three countries and for every one who came there were at least 10 who couldn't. John Beecher wasn't there as his excursions in Dallas and Lubbock for the movie premieres ("The Buddy Holly Story") had taken too much of his money. However, he sent a tape which Bill Griggs played on Saturday morning. Bill Griggs looks almost exactly like J. P. Richardson, crew-cut and all. Bill's wife, Mary, helps him with every aspect of the fan dub, and they are both warm, wonderful people. Mary Griggs operated the selling table, selling records, t-shirts, songbooks, photos, etc., during every break and did a very brisk business. Bill has a room in his basement devoted to Buddy. Over 500 LP's filed by country, photos, tapes, singles, recording equipment, etc.

I arrived in Hartford, Friday evening, Aug. 25th, and Bill picked me up and a Canadian girl, Liz Mikel, at the hotel lobby about 8 PM and took us to his house to show us his Holly room and play a tape of unreleased Holly stuff (which is great!) Mary was at the airport when we got to Bill's house. After we saw Bill's Holly room, he played for us a video tape of Bud (about 20 seconds) from the Dick Clark special (twice). I sat on the floor in front of Bill's TV and just about swooned over Buddy! Then Mary arrived with the house guest she's gone to the airport to pick up. Niki Sullivan! I still can't believe it! I got my picture taken with Niki! We all talked and listened to the tape of undubbed Holly songs. Then Liz and I had to go back to the hotel about 10 PM as the next group of guests was due at Bill's house.

Saturday morning, we met in the cocktail lounge of the Ramada Inn, the only place available for us at the time. The executive board was introduced individually and spoke. Bill played John Beecher's tape at this time. Niki Sullivan was introduced and spoke. Everyone had a camera and tape recorder. There were never less than 20 or 30 flash bulbs going off at any one time, and often more. Also the whole convention was filmed, mostly by George Nettleton of New York and Dave Skinner of England. Wayne Jones presented the surprise collection to Bill. Bill was completely taken by surprise and was so touched he was in tears. The collection was almost $900. We could buy raffle tickets for prizes. There were several drawings for prizes during Saturday and Sunday. I won only once - a set of 3 UK Holly EP's. First ticket drawn got first choice of prizes for that drawing, and so on till all the prizes for that time were taken. Prizes included records, T-shirts, posters, songbooks, letters from Maria and Niki, pieces of Buddy's birthplace, some photos, etc.

Saturday afternoon, who should show up but Jerry Allison, Joe B. Mauldin, and Sonny Curtis! All of the original Crickets (except Buddy) were there! Oh boy! Dick Jacobs, who produced Bud's New York string sessions, was also there. I got all of their autographs. Those guy's got writer's cramp signing autographs.

Saturday evening we went into another room for dinner. Afterwards, the Crickets sat up front with their bottles of beer and answered questions. They acted more like looney teenagers than middle-aged men. They were having the time of their lives and enjoying it as much as we were.

The dinner broke up around 9:30 PM. Bill had arranged for a midnight showing of the movie for us and all who were going were to meet in the hotel lobby at 11 PM. Well, about 30 - 50 of us gathered in the 3rd floor lobby, and Walter Reynolds of Rhode Island played Holly songs on his acoustic guitar and some of us sang along until the hotel manager asked us to quit. Reynolds can play guitar Holly style with the down strokes and he is quite good. By now, it was almost time to go to the movie, so we wandered on down to the lobby and waited around talking till Wayne Jones got everybody together and he led a caravan of cars to the theater which was several miles away. About 50 - 75 people went to the showing. Some had never seen the movie before. It was my sixth time. Well, I got to bed at 3 AM. I understand that there was another songfest until 4:30 AM, but I had to get some sleep.

Sunday morning we met in the same room as the night before. Bill presented a slide show with recorded narration (the slide show was on Buddy, of course). Hopefully, he will sell photos from this show in the future. And then he showed two film clips. One was of the Crickets on the Ed Sullivan show (without sound) taken from someone's TV (probably in England). It was great, though, just watching Buddy move. The other film was even more poorly filmed. It was a very short footage of a home movie made in Lubbock in the summer of 58. It showed Buddy, Jerry, and Joe clowning around and pretending to fight. Bud was wearing a white sweat shirt, sunglasses, and his motorcycle cap. The film really brings home how slender Buddy was. ([Gary] Busey, in contrast, is a little taller and heavier. Busey is 6' 2"[1.88 meters] and weighs 165 lb. [74.84 kilograms]. Buddy was 5' 11" [1.80 meters] and weighed 145 lb. [65.77 kg]). Busey moves nice in the movie, but I'd much rather watch Buddy Holly himself

After a lunch break, we had a rock band play Holly songs. The Crickets! on borrowed instruments (mostly Bill's). It took them quite a while to set up. Then they played for 25 minutes, I got it on tape. Sonny did a solo of a song he's written about the movie. ['Real Buddy Holly Story']. They were great and loud! The Crickets live in concert! Rhythm guitar - Niki Sullivan; drums - Jerry Allison; electric bass - Joe B Mauldin; lead guitar and vocals - Sonny Curtis. Whoa!

During all these times, there were long breaks during which we milled around, got acquainted, bought things, exchanged addresses, etc. There were also the raffle drawings for prizes. There was every conceivable variety of Holly T-shirts from the official fan club ones that Mary Griggs was selling to hand-painted ones made individually.

The convention adjourned about 4:30 or 5 PM, Sunday. It was off to the airport, bus station, or preparing for a long drive home for most people. I got a ride to the airport with one of the people I'd met there and waited around for my flight to Chicago. [Ultimate destination was Tacoma, WA, where my then-husband was stationed at Fort Lewis]. Yet, I feel that somehow Buddy Holly was there and maybe even enjoyed the convention as much as we, his fans, did.

Sue Frederick

The first time I ever heard the Crickets mentioned was one Sunday, when I was waiting to go into church. Two girls, one of whom I was getting a bit interested in, were standing together and talking. I walked towards them and as I got near I heard the one I wasn't interested in ask the other "Have you heard that record by The Crickets called 'That'll be the day'? It's very good, and the other side is good as well." I immediately decided I would listen out for that song, but I don't remember where I first heard it. It may well have been on Radio Luxembourg, a European radio station that played tapes made in the UK of records being played by UK disc-jockeys. Two big problems with it - the signal was poor and it faded and drifted, and they never played the whole record, only about half of it!!

I do remember that it was thanks to this station that I first heard Buddy Holly singing 'Peggy Sue'. A friend's uncle would tape the late night shows, and my friend and I were listening to a tape one day, probably a Saturday, when 'Peggy Sue' blasted out of the speaker. Wow, I had never heard anything like that before. I sat their dumb-struck as the signal faded and drifted and the record was cut off before the end. I decided that I had to buy the record just as soon as I could.

Buddy's Music

It had to be a mixture of his voice and the music that first caught my attention. Then, the lyrics of the songs were just simple, but good - fairly easy to learn!! Finally, there were those unknown `ingredients' that make you like one singer more than another. I'm not sure, but maybe it was something to do with the way he used and changed the tone of his voice as he sang, and so introduced his personal feelings into the songs, like sincerity and uncertainty - maybe! Whatever it was I came to feel close to him, as if he was a friend - he knew me and I felt that I knew him.

If I was feeling down and low, I'd play his records and the songs would always make me feel much better. If I was feeling good, his songs lifted me even higher!
The big thing about his records was you got two 'a' sides for the price of one! The songs on the 'b' side were really top class songs. So, as a teenager with meagre funds, struggling to buy records, I always thought his records were the best value, by far!

Ritchie's Music

I did and still do like Ritchie's recordings. I thought 'Come on let's go' was a great record, although I didn't buy it at the time -probably no money to spare! It was a powerful, driving, rocking song and I always got a 'buzz' when I heard it on the radio. The song was covered in the UK by a London guy called Tommy Steele, and his version was awful, just awful. It totally lacked the raw energy and spontaneity of Ritchie's, although it did get into the Top 10. I did buy 'Donna', when it was issued - a lovely song, with the great `La Bamba' on the other side.

I think my favourite by Ritchie is 'That's my little Suzie'. A rocking good song, full of warmth and fun!!

The Bopper's Music

I didn't mind listening to 'Chantilly lace' when it was played on the radio, but I never bought the record. I was not a fan, and didn't care for his novelty records. I remember that my mum liked the song!

My wife and I saw the Big Bopper Jnr perform some years ago, and my wife asked me to look out for a Big Bopper CD. Now, when I heard some of his early, straight songs, which were in an easy rocking, strolling style, on the 'Best of....' CD I found, I enjoyed them and thought they were very good. I wish I had heard them years ago!

I still admire and appreciate all the good songs that were written and recorded by these artists. They were very talented musicians. If they had continued in the music business, I'm sure all three would have been very successful, although making their own records may not have been their number one priority.

The recordings they made still sound as good as ever, and they have brought me so much pleasure over the years. They are so full of life and energy I can't imagine ever getting tired of them - they are part of my life!

The tragic accident that occurred on February 3rd 1959 happened just three days after my 15 birthday. It's something I will never forget.

Peter Gibson, Harrow, UK.

It would be easy to dismiss The Big Bopper as a one-hit novelty hero but that simply wasn't the case. The fact that he had 3 hot 100 hits chart in less than a year erases the one hit label swiftly. But he was a wonder; he had written two number 1 hits, a country number one with White Lightning and a pop number one with Running Bear. Who knows what else he had in the works for the world??

He also managed to become a top disc jockey and raise a family while balancing a rock and roll career that was just it its infancy. After having spoken to close to a hundred fans who attended all those original Winter Dance Party shows, one thing is for sure, Ritchie tore up the stage with his guitar and his moves, Buddy was looked upon as a straight up Rock and Roll God, and The Big Bopper made the kids laugh and laugh and laugh, not an easy task in one of the coldest winters in decades in the Midwest. More importantly, JP made his fellow tour members laugh on those long, lonely and freezing hours between gigs. And eventually he would make them all cry for good reason

I'm not a fan of Ritchie and The Big Bopper because they were also on that plane, along with Buddy Holly. I'm a fan because their songs make me smile and because they left an indelible mark on the rock and roll world......

Sevan Garabedian

I remember hearing rock and roll during 1955 and 1956 but it took until 1957 before I realized I liked it. The music was so different from anything that I had ever heard before.

However, it was Buddy Holly who was the greatest influence. It seems that he alone of all the established rock and roll superstars was doing musical experimentation, not to pass beyond rock and roll, but to expand the genres limits.

Sue Frederick

Buddy was the consummate professional. He was a shy gentleman, who knew what he wanted and could captivate his audience from the moment he stepped on stage.

Jim McCool

I am 18 years old and I've always loved oldies music because I basically grew up listening to it. I've always liked the three stars and I always knew of their tragic story but I never really paid too much attention to it. Now, ever since the 50 year anniversary of the fatal crash, I've been getting into their music deeply. And I can honestly say that I love it. They were all so talented and amazing. It's such a shame that they all died so young, before they had a chance to achieve their highest level of greatness. I know that their story as well as their music has a big effect on me and I know I will love it forever and that it'll live on forever.

Addle Laccino (2009)

The impact that Buddy, Ritchie, the Bopper and all the 50's (& early 60's) music had is acknowledged by the fact and success of the Surf Ballroom, Clear Lake, I.A, annual event, which is attended by people from all over the world, and is still going strong 50 years later. That really speaks for itself.

George Tomsco (The Fireballs)

When Buddy hit it big it was really big in the panhandle of Texas. I was attending Amarillo High School at the time. There was band called the Night Hawks and all they played was Buddy Holly and rock-a-billy music. I decided I wanted to do the same.
I started learning how to play the guitar and soon after put my own band together and started playing the music of the time. My drummer, Gary Swafford, started playing drums for the Norman Petty Trio.
It was through this association that I met Norman Petty. I signed with Norman in 1958 and started my own career. Norman put me together with the Fireballs and the rest is history.
I don't believe any of this would have happened without Buddy Holly's success.

Jimmy Gilmer (The Fireballs) 2009

'Buddy Holly ' - The minute I heard "That'll Be The Day" on the radio back in 1957 I knew it was a hit. I went right out and bought the record. From that point on because the sound was so unique I became a fan and anxiously awaited and bought each new release from Buddy and the Crickets. I saw all of the appearances on Dick Clark, Ed Sullivan, and Arthur Murray television shows. It is a real shame that Buddy's appearance on Dick Clark's Saturday Night TV show is missing from the files. Buddy did "Heartbeat" on that show.

Big Bopper - I grew up in Houston, Texas which is relatively close to the Beaumont-Port Arthur area. One Saturday I was watching a locally produced television bandstand program that originated from KGUL-TV (Channel 11) then in Galveston, Texas. Appearing on that show was the Big Bopper who lip synced "Purple People Eater Meets Witch Doctor" the original "A-side" to "Chantilly Lace." Next time I was in a store that sold records I saw that song on a bright yellow "D" record label. Being a fan of independent record labels I bought the song and discovered that I liked the flip side much better than the original "A-side." Later the local record was released nationally on the Mercury label.

Ritchie Valens - I thought "Donna" was an OK song but when the DJs flipped the record over and started playing "La Bamba," that got my attention. I can remember seeing Ritchie on a Hollywood talent show before "American Bandstand" moved from Philadelphia. I believe the show was hosted by a DJ named Sam Riddle. I audio taped the performance and regret now that back in my youth all I was interested in was the music and not the talk. I wish I had recorded the interview!

Bud Buschardt (2009)

I am originally from Big Spring Texas. Back in the late 1950's there was a local country music television show that featured local musicians, Ben Hall and the Circle 4 Ramblers. I watched them every Saturday afternoon. Ben Hall, the leader of the group, also was a songwriter and operated a local recording studio there in Big Spring. He performed a song he penned for Buddy Holly "Blue Days, Black Nights" on that television show- and that was my first introduction to Buddy and his music.

Cary C Banks

My name is Brett Lowden and I am a musician in upstate NY. When I was a little kid, my aunt Lonna used to babysit me, and my very first clear memory is listening to "Everyday" on her little 45 rpm Elvis record player. I have a dim memory of seeing "Oh Boy" on Ed Sullivan, but it was long ago, and I was really little. I can't really remember Feb 3d, but I knew that Buddy had passed away. I recall seeing the first Freddie and the Dreamers LP, and saying "that guy is trying to dress up like Buddy Holly"

In the following years, all the 45's I heard as a kid were lost, and I didn't hear Buddy for a long time. I started playing guitar in the 60's, and eventually started seeking out Buddy's records. It was an adventure, as they were very hard to come by. I began ordering imports from the UK and Germany, and eventually got an OK collection.

I found that the records were better than any instruction for me as far as learning to play guitar. All you had to do was be in tune, and play along with Buddy, and the guitar would reveal its secrets to you. There are still things he did that I can't play, he was amazing!
I met a British keyboard player at a show one night and he heard me doing my Buddy Holly songs. He struck up a conversation with me, and it turned out that he is Dave Adams, a 'Joe Meek' session player, songwriter and recording artist. We have worked together for many years, playing and recording. Dave is one of my very best friends. Buddy has given me an awful lot. He taught me to play music, and made it so that I met most of my closest friends. He gave me a way to feed myself and make a living, and I owe the man a lot. I still think he is the greatest of ALL of them!

Brett Lowden

Were you there?

I heard a record on the jukebox , just the other day
And standing there was Johnny, with his ducktail and blue suedes.
He said Buddy sang this, back in '58
When I saw him with the Crickets, and man, they were great

I said did you hear him sing Peggy Sue
Rave On and I'm Gonna Love You Too ?
Well, I wish I could have been there, to hear him sing
Oh, Boy, I bet they really made the rafters ring

Chorus
And did he play his Fender guitar?
And did he look like a rock n roll star?
Or was he more just like the boy next door?
And when they finished playing, did the crowd yell out for more?

I was eight years old when the Big Bopper died. In 1959, television, radio and records were not easy accessible for the average eight year old. In spite of that, Chantilly Lace was a song that I knew by heart. To have "a pretty face and a pony tail" was a definite goal for all young girls.

Like so many others, I wonder about how their lives would have continued had they not died so young. They all seem to have been destined to live their lives immersed in music. The more you know about their lives the more you appreciate what they accomplished.

Swanette A Smith (2009)

Music today seems to be more of an ego thing than the togetherness that music from the first days of rock 'n' roll expressed. It appears that many of today's artists want to create as many parts as they can on their records. Technology allows the layering or stacking of tracks. When you listen to recording session outtakes with Elvis, Buddy, the Beatles, Beach Boys and others from the era, you can hear the musicians and producers offering suggestions.

Everyone contributed to the artistic creation of the product. I feel that too much of today's music is made to fit a formula. Buddy, Bopper, and Valens with his producer Bob Keene were pioneers and leaders.

Bud Buschardt

Local author Gary Clevenger says Holly left a cultural impact in other ways.

Clevenger is editing a book of essays about Holly, the Big Bopper, Valens and pilot Roger Peterson, who also died in the plane crash.

Clevenger says John Lennon was reluctant to perform while wearing his glasses — until he saw footage of Holly in concert while wearing his signature horn-rimmed glasses.

Howard Kramer, a curator at the Rock and Roll Hall of Fame and Museum in Cleveland, agrees with Clevenger that Holly may have been rock's first Every Man.
"Chuck Berry was very cool with the thin mustache and he was a showman," Kramer says. "Buddy was this tall guy and he wore those glasses. People saw him and felt that they could (make music), too.

Billy McGuigan says the common man sensibility that Holly brought to the music can be heard in the energy of rock music.

Howard Dukes

Roger Arthur Peterson

Greater Men May Have Lived But I Doubt It

High School Attended: Fairview High School

Basketball Team (1953-1954) Wins 13 / Losses 8

Baseball Team (Third Base)

Batting Average .478

Roger was also active on the school newspaper / drama club (Fairview High School)

Nickname: Supe

Voted Prettiest Hair while attending Fairview High School

http://en.wikipedia.org/wiki/Roger_Peterson_(pilot)

Jim Fredrickson's eyes mist up when he thinks of Roger Peterson, his former student. "What a great kid," he said.

Peterson is remembered as the 22-year-old pilot who died along with Buddy Holly, Ritchie Valens and J.P. Richardson ("The Big Bopper") when their plane crashed near Clear Lake in February 1959.

"He was at my basketball game the night he crashed," said Fredrickson, 82, who spent 30 years as a teacher, athletic director and coach at what became Rockwell-Swaledale High School before he retired in 1988.

Prior to that, he taught history and coached at Fairview High School in Alta where Peterson was one of his students and athletes.

Fredrickson browsed through an old yearbook and pointed out photographs of Peterson and his future wife, DeAnn Lenz.

"Roger was a good baseball player and fair at basketball," he said.
Fredrickson also spotted a photo of himself and laughed at the full head of dark hair.
"I used to run a comb through my hair. Now I run my hair through a comb," he said with a laugh.

He has fond memories of Roger and his future wife in school at Fairview.
"They were in my history class and they used to wink at each other during class," he said. "I don't know whether I'd let them get away with that today, but back then, I did. I wasn't that much older than they were and, heck, I married my high school sweetheart," he said.
Fredrickson said Peterson was the son of a pilot and from time to time the boy would fly to the high school from his rural home.
"He didn't have a license back then but he knew how to fly. He'd land his plane in the pasture next to the school.

"When he went home, if it was getting dark, his father would shine his car lights in the area where he was going to land," he said. When the Fredricksons moved to Rockwell, Peterson kept in touch with them and stayed at their home when he came to Mason City and applied for a job as a charter pilot for the Dwyer Air Service.

Fredrickson said he and his wife were also friends with Petersons's parents.

"His folks would come to visit us after the crash. With all the attention given to those who died, you could tell they didn't think Roger got a fair shake in the media," he said.

"When I heard the news about the crash on the radio, I was just crushed," said Fredrickson.

"But you know, when you've been in education for over 40 years, you lose a lot of kids. I've had kids killed in Vietnam and in plane crashes and car accidents and suicides.
"And you know what? They're all crushing."

Leave It In The Hands Of Fate
© 1992, Andy Wilkinson, Cain't Quit Music, Inc. (BMI)

Well, I never knowed that it snowed in Hell
But it was snowin' like Hell that night,
When a young singer called me up
Lookin' for a charter flight.
He said, "The bus, you know, is just a little too slow,
And I hadn't got time to wait,"
He said, "A man's gotta do what has gotta be done
And leave it in the hands of fate,
Leave it in the hands of fate."

Now, I'm no fool as a general rule
And the first rule in stayin' alive
Is that a winter storm up in Iowa
Is a damn fool time to fly.
I didn't want to go and I told him so
But he said he just couldn't be late,
He said, "A man's gotta do what has gotta be done
And leave it in the hands of fate,
Leave it in the hands of fate."

Yeah, I should'a stayed home but I liked his songs,
Especially "Peggy Sue."
Besides, he was a star and I was a pilot
And we both had jobs to do.
And we was the kind, when we set our minds,
Never looked back on mistakes,
Because a man's gotta do what has gotta be done
Then leave it in the hands of fate,
Leave it in the hands of fate.

Well, you gotta believe what you can't understand;
Destiny, it ain't in our hands.
Everything plays a part in the plans
Written in the hands of fate,
Written in the hands of fate.

What will be is the truth to me,
Not anything that might have been.
And everybody's got a path to walk,
The famous and the common men.
Our paths crossed in a killing frost
In a cornfield near Clear Lake,

I wrote the song because I felt it unfair that Roger Peterson had been so completely ignored by Buddy's fans and historians.

I never knew Buddy; though we grew up in the same town, I was too much younger than him. I had friends, however, whose older siblings knew him well, and from what I've heard from them, and from what I've learned since from others who knew him as well as anyone could -- his musician pals, J. I and Joe B. and Sonny, etc. -- I get the sense that Buddy himself would be appalled that Peterson would be so dismissed.

Was the crash due to pilot error? Almost certainly. But Peterson was young, just like his passengers, and surely filled with the same sense of the daring of the moment that impelled his fares to risk flying on such a day.

To use a phrase favored by test pilots of the time, we all push the envelope when we're in our twenties and full of piss and vinegar and fortified with the mantle of the invincibility of youth.

Given that, and the entreaties of the popular and charismatic singers who sought him out for the flight, how could one not take the chance to help out Buddy?

Peterson, in that sense, was as much victim as the others. Someone needed to speak up for him, and giving voice to the silent is what we folk singers do best.

Andy Wilkinson 2009

Buddy was spending the night at the house. When it was time to pick up us kids at school both my dad and Buddy came to pick us up. My brother and I, we jumped into the back seat of our car, Buddy riding shotgun....Well, my brother wanted to show off Buddy to his friends that refused to believe that Buddy was our cousin ...... So my brother begged my dad to stop at this boy's house so he could meet Buddy himself, and would once and for all believe that Buddy was our cousin.

Our dad drove us over there. My brother jumped out of the car and ran as fast as he could to the boy's front door....The boy answered..... My brother brought the boy to the car. Buddy rolled down the window, and said "Hi, I'm Buddy Holley ". The boy was shocked and shook his hand, my brother, said "See, I told ya he was my cousin - I told you, I told you, I told you.

When my brother finally got back in the car, Buddy, said: Did you tell him??? Are you sure you told him?????

Well we all had a good laugh over that one.

Buddy said "Wonder if I should write a song called 'I told you, I told you, I told you!!!!' "as he was playing drum sounds on his knee.

Donna Burgess

The Bopper gave the impression of power and comedy, as well as a good rockin' sound.

Kenneth Coombes

Buddy's songs are unique; I listen to the timeless music from my childhood without ever getting tired. As a radio fan I listened to Buddy's music starting in 1958, Peggy Sue was my favorite song.

Hans Werner Finking

I discovered the music when I was about 12 years old. The movie La Bamba really opened my eyes to it. After that I developed a growing appreciation for the music that I now consider the best ever!!

Jim McCool

I think of Ritchie Valens, Buddy Holly and JP, The Big Bopper, and I can't help but think of all the great songs and contributions we missed out on because they were on that plane in 1959.

Sevan Garabedian

I liked the Big Bopper more from a novelty angle at first, the way he put over the lyrics in an almost black jive talk. Later of course I realized what a talented guy he was as a songwriter.

John Firminger

BUDDY HOLLY LIVES ON IN LUBBOCK!!!

The Second Buddy Holly International Convention & Memorial Concert
September 6 - 8, 1979, Lubbock, Texas

At Don Larson's invitation, I flew to Denver to join his Denver-to-Lubbock car caravan. Arrived in Denver early in the morning of Tuesday, Sept. 4. Don, Barb Rau, and Penny Sue Falker (Don's other house guests) picked me up at the airport, and we visited a couple of record stores in Denver, then drove to the Larson house in Evergreen, 30 miles away. Met Don's charming wife Kay and their two children, Bryan and Krista.

We spent much of the 4th getting ready for the 500-mile ride to Lubbock, via Clovis. Tues. evening, Don gave Barb, Penny Sue, and I a preview of his Buddy Holly slide show (which is quite good) while we got half plastered on the Larsons' fabulous concoction - brandy slush. During the evening, we also made signs to put on Don's car.

Early in the morning of Wed, Sept. 5, just after six, Denver time, all five of us adults (the Larson kids were staying with neighbors while their parents were on vacation) and our luggage piled into the Larson's station wagon and took off. Just south of Denver, we picked up John and Angel Perkins of Vail. I transferred briefly to their car to help relieve congestion in Don's car. At Colorado Springs, we were joined by Donn Lowe. As Donn was traveling alone, I again switched cars, so Donn could have someone to keep him company and help him stay awake. At Santa Rosa, New Mexico, we were joined by Marianne Curson and her friend Jim Gilbert, of Phoenix, and by Mike Oestreicher of Flagstaff; two more cars with Holly signs and stickers and Mike's "Rave On" license plate. That completed the caravan with 5 cars and 11 people.

On the trip between Santa Rosa and Clovis, we were frequently buzzed by the New Mexico fuzz. The police cars would pass us and even get in between the cars briefly. Apparently, the highway patrol was passing word around about the weirdoes with all those Buddy Holly signs, and all the fuzz along our route wanted to see the traveling freak show.
We arrived in Clovis about 5 PM, New Mexico time. The old Nor-Va-Jak studio buildings are on the main highway, and Norman Petty lives behind them (he currently has a studio downtown). We all parked on a side street, and Don Larson (who knows Petty personally) went to see if Norman was home. We had to wait about 30 minutes till Mr. Petty arrived (he had been busy elsewhere). When he did arrive, he apologized for not being able to let us in the old studio as it was being used for storage and was in total disarray. However, Mr. Petty very graciously stood out on the grass between the two buildings and permitted us to get our pictures taken with him and to get his autograph. We found Norman Petty to be a friendly, courteous person who patiently put up with all our questions and autograph and picture requests. All in all, it was quite an honor and pleasure to meet this man who contributed so greatly to Buddy's music.

We spent about an hour in Clovis and then drove to Lubbock. We arrived at the Villa Inn about 9 PM, Lubbock time, quite tired. But Bill Griggs was there, and then Niki Sullivan came, so many of us stayed up quite late Wed. night. I shared a room with Lisa Hennes of Seattle, the other Washington state member to come. Then I and my family lived in Tacoma, WA, as my now ex-husband was stationed at Fort Lewis

On Thursday, Sept. 6, after people had finally woke up and watched TV. At 8:45, Waylon Jennings was on a local talk show, talking about Buddy, and then at 9 and 11:30, Bill and Niki were on different shows, together.

Then Don Larson organized a 6-car, 20-person group for a tour of Lubbock. First, we went to KLLL studios which are at a different location than when Buddy used to stop in to listen to records and talk to the staff. The current staff of KLLL was very friendly and give us a tour of their studios. They also mentioned over the air that we were there and played for us the station breaks that Buddy had recorded for them.

After leaving KLLL, we located a florist shop and all chipped in for a bouquet for Buddy. Took a while for the bouquet to be made up, but the wait was well worth it as the wreath was very beautiful with blue ribbons which read in gold letters "Buddy Holly Memorial Society".

Then came our trip to the City of Lubbock Cemetery. We parked about a block from the entrance for a while and listened to a KLLL interview with Niki Sullivan. Upon conclusion of the interview, we drove into the cemetery and parked across the narrow road from Buddy's grave, which is next to the road. This is always the hardest part for me during any trip to Lubbock. It's so hard to believe that Buddy Holly could be there under that stone. It just doesn't seem possible that such a vital, dynamic, creative person could be gone. It does not seem possible that Buddy Holly is dead, and yet he is and for 20 years.
Kay Larson put the bouquet on the grave. There were already 3 or 4 other offerings of flowers there. We took pictures and some of us may have shed a few quiet, private tears over the loss of this incredible man.

After leaving the cemetery, we went to KDAV, which is now called KRLB. We were met in the parking lot by one of the staff carrying a tape recorder, and he asked us where we all were from. The radio station is still in the same building as it was when Buddy and Bob had their show there, but so extensively remodeled that the only thing left from Buddy's time is a control board (which he sometimes used). Like the staff of KLLL, the people at KRLB were very warm and friendly. Indeed, we found this same warmth and gracious Texas hospitality from virtually the entire population of Lubbock. Almost all of us crowded into the broadcast room and were on the air. Don Larson was our spokesman and he explained who we were and why we were in Lubbock. Graham Harrison of England also spoke briefly; then Don introduced us all and said where each one came from.

From KRLB, we went to the Cotton Club outside the Lubbock city limits, where Buddy used to play. [I think now that the building we saw may not have been the original]. The Cotton Club is closed, and the building is deteriorating. There was a liquor store next door and some of the group stocked up on potables for the party scheduled for that evening. Don Larson did a great job of guiding and keeping together about 20 wall-eyed, excited, camera-laden Holly fans. I don't know how he managed, but he did so admirably.

As it was getting late now, we headed back to the hotel, stopping by a grocery store on the way to stock up on food for the party.

I ate supper at the hotel Thur. evening (food and sleep came in a poor second behind running around Lubbock, talking to other Holly fans, and buying pictures, etc., from Bill Griggs and Don Larson) with a group of about 12 people including Bill Griggs, John Goldrosen, and John's constant companion, Liz Mikel of Canada. At about 9 PM, the birthday party for Buddy commenced in room 246, that of Barb Rau and Penny Sue Falker. Imagine 30 or 40 people crowding into an average sized hotel room. Wall-to-wall people really raised the room temperature, and some people had to go out on the walkway every so often to cool off. There were drinks and food. Walter Reynolds of Rhode Island brought an electric guitar along and played Holly songs, and we all sang along, loudly. Niki and Fran Sullivan showed up. Niki played a lot, too. Most of the time it was either Walter or Niki playing Holly songs on the guitar, and most of the rest of us singing at the top of our lungs. John Goldrosen was there all the time and I think he sang every song. Lisa Hennes, 16, showed up us older folk, by staying there the whole time and knowing the words to every song. We made up in enthusiasm what we lacked in talent. There was always a small group on the walkway outside the open door, trying a catch a breath of cooler air before plunging back into the mass of warm bodies. We all stopped singing briefly while Niki sang the calypso version of "Peggy Sue", and a rather risqué song that Buddy sometimes sang. Most of the time from 9 PM to 2 or 3 AM though, we were singing along and enjoying ourselves thoroughly. Then Don Larson presented Niki with a Niki Sullivan collage that Don had made from the photos of Niki taken at the memorial concert in Clear Lake in Feb. Niki and Fran were very touched by this and the collage was excellent as are all of Don's collages. After this the music resumed until a few minutes past midnight; as it was now Sept. 7, Kay Larson lit candles (43) on a cake, and we all sang "Happy Birthday" to Buddy (I truly hope he had a happy one). Then the music again resumed and gradually slacked off between 2 and 4 AM in the morning.

Friday morning, Sept. 7, after getting 3 or 4 hours of sleep, I went with Dave Garavick of Pennsylvania, Sal La Manna or San Diego, and Lisa Hennes, around Lubbock in Dave's rental car (which had air-conditioning). As Dave had to pick up his concert ticket, we went to the Lubbock Civic Center and saw the auditorium where the concert was scheduled. It's a very new building, only a few years old.

We went and photographed the sign stretching across a downtown street, reading "Buddy Holly Lives on in Lubbock".

After a few unsuccessful attempts to find picture postcards of Lubbock, we finally located the Chamber of Commerce. Here we loaded up on brochures describing Lubbock, Lubbock lapel buttons, street maps, and a 3 page pamphlet on Buddy that John Goldrosen had written for them.

As we arrived back at the hotel, the TV news truck was just pulling away. They had filmed some of the BHMS members in the patio of the Villa Inn, and a small clip was shown on the news that night.

A group of about 6 people went in Walter Reynolds' car to Clovis, leaving about 1 PM on Friday afternoon, and there was some mild concern that they might not get back in time for the concert.

In between running around Lubbock and buying things, small groups would gather on the hotel patio (which is indoors) and talk. There was almost always someone there.
I don't think that there was a roll of blank film left to be bought in Lubbock by Sunday morning. Ditto flash bulbs. The amount of pictures taken by 80 to 100 Holly fans must have been in the thousands.

Not too long after the TV news crew left, Steve Bonner of Dallas was talking to a gray-haired man on the other side of the small swimming pool. Then someone casually mentioned something about Steve getting Tommy Allsup to come to Lubbock. Our brains started putting two and two together; we looked at the man Steve was talking to. Then came the frantic rush for notebooks and cameras. You guessed it; it was Tommy Allsup that Steve was talking to. Liz Mikel rushed up to Don Larson's room and hurriedly bought a copy of the Eau Claire [Wisconsin] picture for Tommy to autograph. He was very friendly and courteous and patiently permitted us to photograph him, and he signed all request autographs.

Then it was time to have a quick supper and get ready for the concert. Yes, the Clovis group got back on time. There were several tables at the Civic Center selling concert programs for $2 each, and color portraits of Buddy. The programs are very beautifully done with that color picture of Buddy on the cover. One of the photos inside was a recently discovered one of Buddy and Waylon taken in one of those do-it-yourself photo machines during the last tour.

Most of the BHMS members were sitting down front (I was in the very first row). The concert was a near sell-out. The concert was late getting started. While we were all waiting, Maria Elena walked by, and someone recognized her. So, of course, out came the notebooks, pictures, cameras, etc. As word rapidly spread that Maria was there, a long line formed down the aisle, and Maria very graciously signed autographs and permitted her picture to be taken for a least half an hour.

The concert started about 20 minutes late. The mayor of Lubbock, Dirk West, made the opening remarks, and then Tony Joe White opened the show. He really has no connection to Buddy. But he really rocked out with songs like 'Polk Salad Annie" and "I get off on it". Really enjoyed his set.

Just before the intermission, Mayor West asked Buddy's parents and Maria Elena to stand up, so during intermission a crowd gathered around Lawrence and Ella Holley's seats. Mr. and Mrs. Holley very good-naturedly signed autographs, as did Maria Elena, who was now seated between Mrs. Holley and Joan Turner.

Then it was time for the Crickets! Jerry, Joe, and Sonny came on stage to thunderous applause. While the Cricket's set was a bit short, it was fantastic! They played several Holly songs as well as Sonny's compositions, "I Fought the Law" and "Love is all around". During the set, Sonny says, "Let's rock and roll'; and the Crickets plunged into a rip-roaring, rockin' and rollin' version of "Slippin' and Slidin'"! This is rock and roll at its very best, the Crickets.

No other rock group can ever be so good! The Crickets still chirp in Lubbock! Can't no music satisfy the soul like that good old rock and roll. Now, if only Buddy could have been there.

Toward the end of the Crickets' set, Waylon Jennings joined them for a Holly medley. Then the Crickets left, and Waylon's group took over. Jennings sang his own songs for quite a while. His fans were a bit overenthusiastic at the end and crowded down front of the stage. He did not close with "Old Friend" as would have been appropriate, nor did the Crickets come back for an encore.

The general consensus that I heard the next morning was too little Crickets, too much Waylon, but the Crickets were fantastic! After the concert, people again crowded around the Holleys and Maria Elena. Buddy's sister Patricia was also there.

Saturday, Sept. 8 at noon, about 80 -100 fans showed up (along with about 6 news photographers) for a memorial service at the cemetery. We all gathered in a semi-circle around Buddy's grave. By now there were still more bouquets of flowers, including one beautiful bunch of red roses from Peggy Sue (yes, the Peggy Sue). Bill Griggs played a tape of Buddy's songs and Buddy talking that he [Bill] had prepared for the service. The tape ended with the Angelic Gospel Choir's recording of "I'll be Alright" - Buddy's favorite gospel song, and the one played at his funeral. Then Bill read a poem he'd written about Buddy. Partway through, Bill broke down crying and had to leave the group. Bill wasn't the only one crying; most of us were. After a few minutes, Bill recovered and finished reading the poem. Buddy's loss hurts us all very deeply. Then Niki Sullivan and his mother each placed a single rose on the gravestone. All of us grieved in our own personal way.
Upon leaving the cemetery, we drove to the Buddy Holly Recreation Area for lunch (which some forgot to bring). After individual picture taking, we all gathered around the name sign for a group picture.

Then Larry Holley, Buddy's brother, showed up and, of course, he was the center of constant attention, non-stop questions, requests for autographs, and picture-taking. Many people had tape recorders and recorded everything but the concert (recorders were not allowed there). Larry Holley is a very warm, friendly person, as, indeed, is the whole Holley family.

They really went out of their way to be nice to us, and we really appreciated it.
Someone made a suggestion that since the whole group could not go to the Holley home, and most of us had never seen or touched anything that had belonged to Buddy, could Larry please bring something of Buddy's - like maybe a pair of glasses - to the hotel for our meeting there after leaving the recreation area. Larry said he might bring what he called Buddy's "diddy bag',' in which Bud carried stuff like his throat medicine (all singers worry about voice trouble). This bag had had its bottom torn out by the plane crash [I think Bill Griggs now has this bag], but the top and sides were still alright The group around Larry Holley did not want to break up to go back to the hotel but finally were compelled to by time.

We were in one of the Villa Inn's hospitality rooms on the first floor. First we had a T-shirt contest, won by Bruce Christensen of Florida. Then a group of us got up, and each tried to name a Holly song title not previously named in the game. If you couldn't, you were out of the game and had to sit down. Then we had a written contest about Holly song titles.

Now here came what had to be the highlight of the convention. Larry Holley showed up with not one, but two of Buddy's guitars, the Stratocaster and the leather-covered Gibson. Larry was wearing two of Bud's rings. He brought a red-plaid flannel shirt of Buddy's (size 15), a hat Buddy used to wear when fishing, a pair of Buddy's shoes (size 8, black with side buckles, bought in England), and a belt Buddy had carved for him. We all got to touch the guitars and have our pictures made with them. The leather-carving on the Gibson is like new (well-taken care of) and excellent. The guy who carved that was really talented! Larry Holley played the Stratocaster and sang, then so did Niki Sullivan (the guitar was not plugged in, so made very little sound).

Mrs. Holley showed up also and she was the center of constant attention. She was accompanied by Joan Turner.

The nervous excitement, the feeling of unreality, of reverence when actually touching something of Buddy's, cannot really be described; it has to be felt. To really be touching something once touched by that incredible man that we all love so deeply.
All the Holleys left, and then Don Larson presented his slide show with taped narration. Then the meeting was over and so was the convention.

All in all, we got to see and touch things we never thought we would. Everything that is, except Buddy.

Sue Frederick

Lubbock High School - 1955

The following three pages show extracts from the Lubbock High School Westerner **Yearbook of 1955. This was the senior year for Buddy Holly.**

VIC of ICT Attends District Convention

Officers are, clockwise, Charlene Hadaway, secretary; Buddy Holly, vice-president; and Delton Combs, president. Not pictured are James Hogan, treasurer; Bob Montgomery, reporter; and Don Adams, sergeant-at-arms.

Nineteen different trades are engaged in by the 36 members of Vocational Industrial Club of Industrial Co-operative Training, Chapter 95. These students work afternoons and have a business meeting once a week.

Socials included a formal initiation at K. N. Clapp Party House and an Employer-Employee Banquet. Tuesday nights the group played basketball or volleyball in the boys' gym.

Representatives went to a district meet in Amarillo and the state meet at Waco. Lawana Hilburn attended these as club sweetheart.

Members are Delton Combs, Buddy Holly, Charlene Hadaway, James Hogan, Bob Montgomery, Don Adams, Sarah Adams, J. C. Alexander, Don Allen, David Bowers, Carolyn Cone, Lawrence Dale, Aubrey Davis, James Fread, Reagan Garrett, Eugene Green, Billy Henson, Lawana Hilburn, Amos Hodge, Henry Housour, George Jones, John Jackson, Wayne Jacobs, Don Ledwig, Bobby Mayfield, Jimmie Oglesby, Beverly Patrick, John A. Petty, James Pritchard, Mary Robertson, Norman Williamson, Frank Wilson, Herbert Wilson, Harold Womack, Eddie Yuzbick, and Ray Nall.

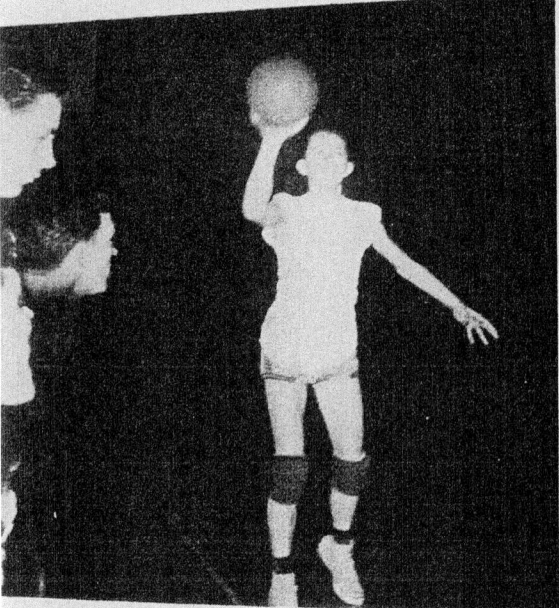

Frank Wilson is taking a free shot in the basketball game held every Tuesday night in the boys' gym. Other members of the club participating in the activity are Aubrey Davis, James Fread, and Bobby Mayfield.

Beverly Patrick is explaining to James Fread, Wayne Jacobs, Harold Womack, John A. Petty, and Aubrey Davis, the correct places for the keywords, *skill, knowledge,* and *experience,* on the club symbol.

CLASS OF 55

LLOYD HATCHETT
JON HATLEY
BOBBY HAYGOOD
MARTHA HAYSLIP

JEROME HENDERSON
JIM HENDERSON
SHERRY HENDRICK
JOY HEROD

NANCY HERRING
WENDELL HESTER
BILLY EARL HEWETT
DENNIS HICKS

GLENN HIGGINBOTHAM
CLAUDETTE HILL
SONDRA HILL
DONOVAN HILLIARD

AMOS HODGE
SARJIM HOLCOMB
BROWN HOLDEN
ROSE MARY HOLDER

JOHN HOLLARS
BUDDY HOLLEY
JERRY HOLTON
STELLA HOLTON

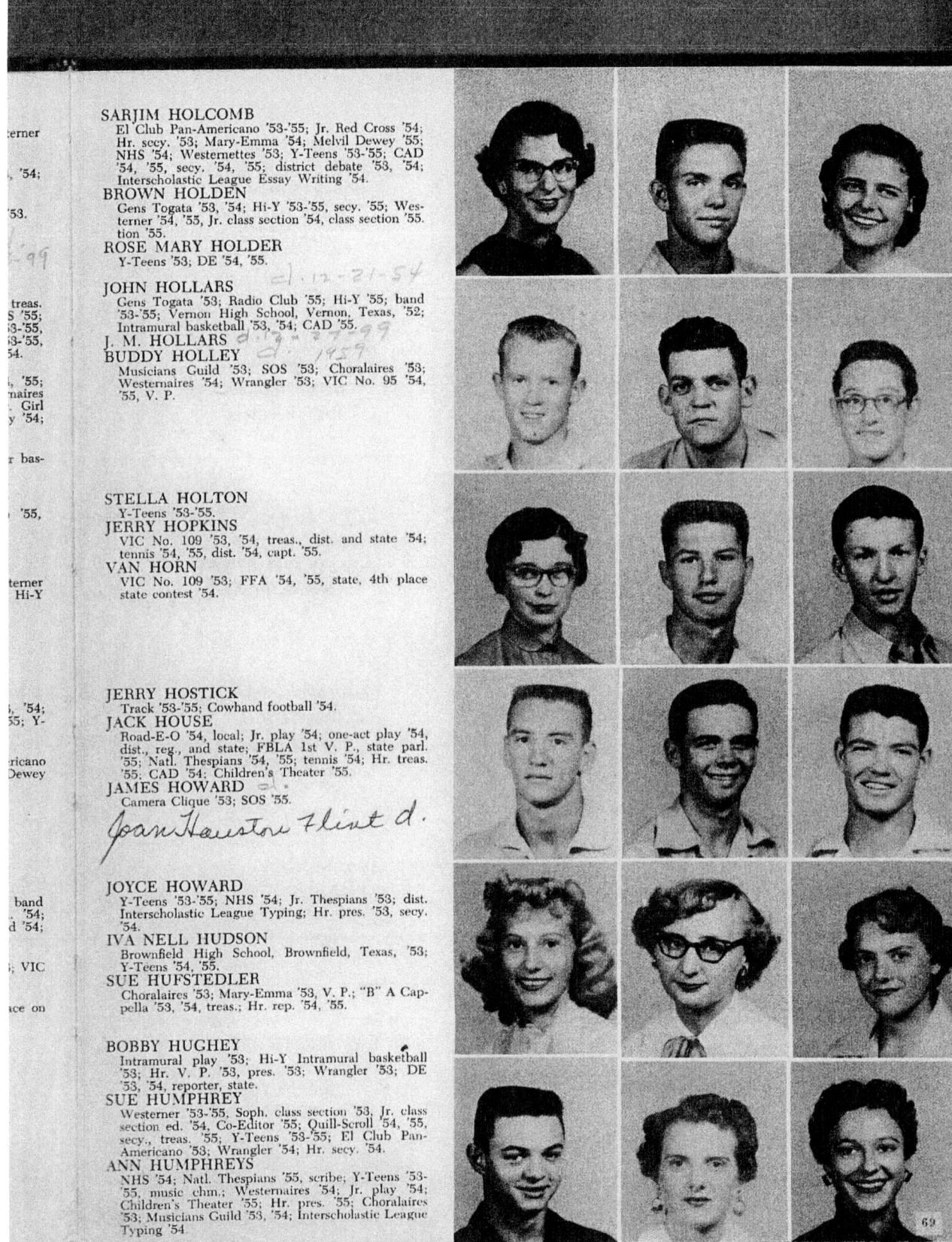

SARJIM HOLCOMB
El Club Pan-Americano '53-'55; Jr. Red Cross '54; Hr. secy. '53; Mary-Emma '54; Melvil Dewey '55; NHS '54; Westernettes '53; Y-Teens '53-'55; CAD '54, '55, secy. '54, '55; district debate '53, '54; Interscholastic League Essay Writing '54.

BROWN HOLDEN
Gens Togata '53, '54; Hi-Y '53-'55, secy. '55; Westerner '54, '55, Jr. class section '54, class section '55. tion '55.

ROSE MARY HOLDER
Y-Teens '53; DE '54, '55.

JOHN HOLLARS
Gens Togata '53; Radio Club '55; Hi-Y '55; band '53-'55; Vernon High School, Vernon, Texas, '52; Intramural basketball '53, '54; CAD '55.

J. M. HOLLARS

BUDDY HOLLEY
Musicians Guild '53; SOS '53; Choralaires '53; Westernaires '54; Wrangler '53; VIC No. 95 '54, '55, V. P.

STELLA HOLTON
Y-Teens '53-'55.

JERRY HOPKINS
VIC No. 109 '53, '54, treas., dist. and state '54; tennis '54, '55, dist. '54, capt. '55.

VAN HORN
VIC No. 109 '53; FFA '54, '55, state, 4th place state contest '54.

JERRY HOSTICK
Track '53-'55; Cowhand football '54.

JACK HOUSE
Road-E-O '54, local; Jr. play '54; one-act play '54, dist., reg., and state; FBLA 1st V. P., state parl. '55; Natl. Thespians '54, '55; tennis '54; Hr. treas. '55; CAD '54; Children's Theater '55.

JAMES HOWARD
Camera Clique '53; SOS '55.

JOYCE HOWARD
Y-Teens '53-'55; NHS '54; Jr. Thespians '53; dist. Interscholastic League Typing; Hr. pres. '53, secy. '54.

IVA NELL HUDSON
Brownfield High School, Brownfield, Texas, '53; Y-Teens '54, '55.

SUE HUFSTEDLER
Choralaires '53; Mary-Emma '53, V. P.; "B" A Cappella '53, '54, treas.; Hr. rep. '54, '55.

BOBBY HUGHEY
Intramural play '53; Hi-Y Intramural basketball '53; Hr. V. P. '53, pres. '53; Wrangler '53; DE '53, '54, reporter, state.

SUE HUMPHREY
Westerner '53-'55, Soph. class section '53, Jr. class section ed. '54, Co-Editor '55; Quill-Scroll '54, '55, secy., treas. '55; Y-Teens '53-'55; El Club Pan-Americano '53; Wrangler '54; Hr. secy. '54.

ANN HUMPHREYS
NHS '54; Natl. Thespians '55, scribe; Y-Teens '53-'55, music chm.; Westernaires '54; Jr. play '54; Children's Theater '55; Hr. pres. '55; Choralaires '53; Musicians Guild '53, '54; Interscholastic League Typing '54.

I had a job at the airport and had put in my first year as a "crop-duster" pilot and Buddy walked into the office. I had made something like $8000 that season and thought I was rich. Buddy told me he had made $188,000 that year with his recordings.

Gerald Martin LHS CLASS OF 55

I knew Buddy. I had a class or two with him. I sang next to him in Choir. He always wanted to sing flat to irritate the director. We sang together in a class called ensemble. The group sang English music like Green Sleeves, etc. He occasionally played his guitar. As a technician, I felt he was as good as any professional. He could make his guitar sing

William Nolan LHS CLASS OF 55

Buddy Holley and I went to see Elvis at the Cotton Club .The second time he came there, Buddy played his Les Paul in Elvis's band the first time. When Elvis took a break he came and sat at our table; some lady asked him why he didn't comb his hair. Elvis asked her why she didn't brush her teeth. I often remember the good times Buddy and I had and I'll always miss him. He will always be my best friend.

Reagen Garrett LHS CLASS 55

My favorite recollection of Buddy is this: The year was 1952. Buddy, Bobby Montgomery, I, and some other sophomores were getting initiated into El Cub Pan Americano (the Spanish club at LHS). We initiates were to perform the program, and I was in charge of the program. Came the big day and I go up to the school. Miss Wilhite, the sponsor, asked me what we were going to do. Then I remembered I was in charge and had done nothing! Luckily, Buddy and Bobby were there. They said, "Don't worry Chalky. We can sing and play the guitar a little bit. We'll go home and get our guitars."
That night El Club Pan-American had the best initiation program they had ever seen. Buddy and Bobby did magnificently!
I like to tell everyone that I gave Buddy his start in show business.

Chalky Strogner LHS CLASS 55

I was in the 35th Cacti and two of the trio were in the 27th Wolfhounds, I think. I think the third was a civilian living on Waikiki. They sang and practiced on Saturday and Sunday afternoons in the Hawaiian Village in a place called the Korean Hut. A large group of GI's were there to drink beer and listen, every weekend. When Buddy toured Hawaii in, I think February '58, I had told one of the trio that I knew Buddy. We went to the concert and tried to get in, but were unsuccessful. Later after the concert and a few drinks, we went to the Royal Hawaiian and I saw someone in the lounge I knew from Lubbock. He called Buddy and we went up to the 4th floor, I think and Buddy met us in the hall. It took those musicians only a few minutes to get going. It was late and got later, but no one complained. The music was great.

William Nolan LHS CLASS 55

Buddy was a very shy type of person that everybody liked and had his own style.
We were in Mrs. Webster's home room together. I was blessed and watched as he and Bobby Montgomery got very popular singing and writing. Our class was a very large class that still has lunch once a month in Lubbock, Dallas, Houston or Austin, Texas
Its fun to get reacquainted with everyone after all these years

Terry Williams LHS CLASS OF 55

Buddy was in elementary school with me, 2nd thru 5th at Roscoe Wilson. The new school split our 6th grade and Buddy left.
Nikki Sullivan, (Crickets) played in the LHS band and were known as "suck-and-blow-boys". The Buddy and Bob (Montgomery)] show early on KDAV mornings was mostly country western. Buddy was not as popular as performers Dunbar Combo.
There was a chinning bar on the Roscoe Wilson playground. We guys always liked to play "war" which was played by attempting to wrap your legs around your opponent and force him to drop from the bar. That always, nearly, ended up in a fight. Buddy would play but he was not very successful and his fights did not last long. School was "catty-corner" from Waggoner Park, home to us all. The fights were staged here to keep from getting in trouble.

Robert Welch LHS CLASS OF 55

It's been a "neat" thing to have had that 'connection' with him, and I think that it has 'connected' our Class. We have a very close relationship with all of us. I do tell a funny story that the reason Buddy didn't sign my annual is because we got into a "squabble" over a mutual girl friend. We decided to 'settle' it "Out Behind The Barn", and Buddy said "I'm gonna kick your ass, Big Boy", and I replied "That'll Be The Day". Strictly a fabricated' story, but I've had a lot of fun with it.

Baxter Lawrence   LHS CLASS OF 55

The one thing I remember about Buddy was we were talking one day and he said "Charlie, one of these days you will be able to tell people you knew Buddy Holley back when.
"I looked at him and said 'Yea B-S"
I believe that was when we were seniors

Chuck Gallimore LHS CLASS OF 55

I didn't really know Buddy that well. My husband knew him and went to the clubs to hear Buddy and his group. They were very popular as Rock and Roll was new and exciting at the time and since Buddy had his own unique twist he was much in demand
I worked with a lady a few years after Buddy died whose son was fortunate enough to be allowed to hang out with the group while they practiced "the sound" in Buddy's garage.

Jean Daniels   LHS CLASS OF 55

I have one little vignette that you may want to use. My family moved from Los Angeles to Lubbock during April 1952, and I was immediately enrolled in the 9th grade at JT Hutchinson Junior High School. As you can imagine this was not the most comfortable day in my life. I didn't know a soul and I was basically a pretty shy guy to begin with. I wandered into a nearby drugstore and found a seat at the soda fountain. After awhile a dark haired fellow with horn-rimmed glasses sat down next to me and introduced himself. He knew I was the new guy in school and welcomed me to Lubbock and JT Hutchinson Junior High School.

So, I am happy to tell you that Buddy Holly was my first friend and school mate in Lubbock. But that's the way Buddy was, just a very nice, quiet, unassuming friendly guy. We remained good friends through out high school

Don Adamson LHS Class of 55

Buddy was not a close friend of mine but we were in a few of the same classes, choir for one and the men's glee club. One of my uncles was a guitar picker and I was learning a few chords from him and displayed my vast knowledge for Buddy a few times. I remember him turning to Bob and saying "See, told you he knows more guitar than us"
Seemed that half the guys in school were scratching around on the guitar, a real hit or miss proposition in those days as there were few teachers back then

Gerald Martin LHS CLASS OF 55

After graduation I did not hear much about him till he toured Hawaii. I was a soldier at Schofield Barracks and knew two of the guys in a new singing trio developing at the Korean Hut on Saturday and Sunday afternoons (Kingston Trio).
I took them to meet Buddy at the concert, but could not get back stage. Later we did catch up with him in the Royal Hawaiian and they sang in the hotel most of the night.

William Nolan LHS CLASS OF 55

I first met Buddy Holly in 7th grade at O.L. Slaton Junior High in Lubbock, Texas. He was in my English class that year. I considered him to be a cute and friendly guy. We moved a few times after that year, so I didn't see Buddy again until 1953 when we were both juniors in Lubbock High School.
I didn't have any classes with Buddy, but he and his band sometime played for our assemblies.
My dad knew his two brothers, Larry and Travis, as they sometime worked together on the same jobs. Larry told the guys that Buddy said he would someday be famous. Indeed he did become famous and still is. I considered it a privilege to have known Buddy.

Barbara Sudduth Newsom LHS Class of 55

Buddy and Bob Montgomery played together and sang each Friday night in high school, mostly on an 18 wheel trailer parked at a park or at a local skating rink that was the hang out then, as well as THE HI-D-HO drive inn just down the street where everybody would go after the shows. I even remember the night Buddy and The Crickets came riding up on their new motor cycles. They were just like the rest of us before. After that they were accepted as stars from Lubbock. I was with Buddy and 2 other guys the night after Elvis had done his first show in Lubbock, he was still driving a truck for a living. We went to a place called the Cotton Club to hang out after the show and Elvis came over to our table to meet Buddy.

Terry Williams LHS CLASS OF 55

I remember Echo McGuire going with him, but no specifics. I remember him, I knew a few of the members of the Crickets, and had classes with one on several occasions. My church MYF was into early rock, but did not connect it to Buddy.
I even helped a guy named Elvis unload syrup for NuGrape soda, but did not make a connection till years later when a friend asked me. He was driving a truck out of the east and sang at the Cotton Club later, after work.
Lubbock had some good music going on at that road spot.

Bill Nolan LHS CLASS OF 55

My fondest memories of the relationship with the Pickerings came in Norman's hand-crafted studio. The day Bill and I sang backup to Rick Tucker with Buddy and the Crickets acting as studio musicians, and Roy Orbison with his brand new bride stopping by to tell of his Sun Records' woes to Norman, only to sit in and go knee-to-knee with Buddy on guitar licks while Bill and I and a guy named Ross Cass warbled in the background.

Bob Lapham

Buddy said we would do that when he returned with the Summer Dance Party with the same crew. He would set that up with the General Artist Corporation when he got back to NYC. Buddy wanted to build in an extra day to water ski at our place and have a bratwurst cookout.
The boys all met their first brats in Green Bay and fell in love with them. Having graduated from the U of Wisconsin and having married a Wisconsin gal, I knew bratwurst !! We had a few in the fridge at all times. So Buddy said "we will do a Summer Dance Party and come a day early".

Bob Hale

Ritchie Valens was injecting a strong Hispanic influence on the genre and was a welcome new star, very talented both as a musician, singer and songwriter. If he had lived his continued influence on rock and roll would have helped keep the music from the semi-stagnation of 1960-1964

Sue Frederick

I will always consider September 7 1936 as The Day The Music Was Born

Gary Clevenger

Ritchie Valens was great to listen to and it would have been interesting to see how far he would have gone in his musical career

Kenneth Coombes

I think of Waylon Jennings and I wonder sometimes if he had gotten on that plane. Think of all the great music the world would have missed out on had he died in 1959. I mean the guys in the Country Hall of Fame

Sevan Garabedian

The first song I heard on the radio was Donna; it impressed me very much

Hans Werner Finking

I am a Ritchie Valens fan. Ritchie packed so much talent into such a short career. He was mature beyond his years and embodied the innocence of the time

Jim McCool

Can it really be fifty years ago, which shows you how talented and influential these guys were.

John Firminger

At school from classmates, some of whom went on to play in groups - one was in the original lineup of Deep Purple - that's when I discovered Buddy Holly's music

Clive Harvey

I first met Buddy when I was about nine or ten. We were both performing in lots of groups. Growing up, music was something to do and we both had lots of fun.

As kids we would go in the backyard of EJ Hollup the football star. We dug caves and had lots of fun, catching pigeons and swimming. When we weren't playing our guitars, we enjoyed doing kid things.

I will always remember the time………..

I got up to sing, I was going to perform solo, and I wasn't doing very good. Next thing I knew Buddy was up on stage with me backing me up. We sounded great after Buddy decided to help me out on stage.

In closing………………………

Buddy got his wish; he got everything he wanted in life, especially the music and recognition. I will always remember my friend. I never forget his Birthday and I choose not to remember his death. Buddy was a good friend.

Tinker Carlen 2009

I was a Buddy Holly fan from day one. I think I bought his first record when I was in the Army. I was a big fan. I came to Marquette Univ in Milwaukee in Jan 1958. I bought all the rock and roll records and everyone knew I had a fabulous huge collection. 45 RPM's then. I lived on 19th St off Wisconsin Ave when the Winter Dance tour was taking place and I saw it advertised. I lived about 6 blocks from the old Eagles Ballroom.

I talked two buddies into going with me. I remember we had good seats. I had the Big Bopper record, it was a novelty record but fun to listen to. I became a Valens fan as soon as I heard his first record and then learned how young he was. The concert was great. Sell out as I recall. I remember going to the back of the Eagles Ballroom to watch the stars board busses and we saw them come out one by one.

There was a big crowd back there. We yelled their names and Holly waved to us and Ritchie came over and shook hands. I got to shake his hand but no autograph. We saw them all leave and board busses.

The day of the plane crash I came home from classes at 3 PM and turned on my radio. I had no TV. I could not believe my ears. I was in shock. That was the first news I had of the crash, and all on the plane were dead. I sat down at my table and I cried like a kid. I had my ticket stub for the show for many years and a copy of the program that I bought at the Eagles Ballroom. I lost them over the years.

I have never stopped remembering these wonderful artists, recording stars. I would say I was most inclined to Buddy Holly. He sang the songs I liked.

Larry Giantomas (2009)

Being brought up on music from the early days of radio before TV and listening to all the great ballad singers on Radio Luxembourg and first record (78) I bought in 1954 'ish of Sammy Davis Jnr 'Because of you'---'It was my life' —then the birth of Rock'n'Roll with Bill Haley—Rock Around The Clock and Elvis came in to contention—then of course Buddy Holly.

Me and two mates—Johnny Whitely and Pete Bryan were all keen record buyers and used to go to Pete's bungalow in Redding's Lane in Greet and discuss each other's discs brought along.

Of course Buddy Holly came in to scenario and all became great fans so when he was booked at Brum Town hall we had to go. We didn't get our tickets till late and only tickets left were on the stage behind the performers—actually on the stage so of course we had to have those tickets.

I remember—master of ceremonies / compere was Des O'Connor--On the bill was Gary Miller—remember his green suit and ginger/red hair who had many ballad hits— The Tanner Sisters ---Ronnie Keene orchestra was also on the bill but can't remember them at all---Well you don't do you ? Buddy Holly was on the bill---Although his set was a blur—I can always remember the fantastic sound of his guitar---it just filled the whole area with an incredible sound—He was a pioneer in the development of the Fender Stratocaster.

From what I can remember—coz it was early days and Buddy didn't have that many songs of his own material I reckon he sang rock 'n' roll hits of other artists—Like to know if anyone has got song line up---but what an experience to actually be on the same stage as Buddy Holly and witnessing this great man perform—no mountains of speakers just the sheer excitement of that voice and guitar sound.

Nothing can beat it although I've seen many great performers since that day 50 years ago. Starting with my first concert at Brum Hippodrome with The Canadian Group
The Crew Cuts in early 50's — Eddie Cochran, Gene Vincent, Little Richard, Roy Orbison, Stax tour with Otis Redding, Sam and Dave, Booker T etc through to Celine Dion in Vegas, Tina Turner, Lionel Ritchie, Josh Groban, ELO, Andrea Bocelli etc.

The list goes on forever but the one that stands out right at front was that BUDDY HOLLY SHOW at TOWN HALL in 1958 !

Danny Reddington 2009

I first heard Buddy Holly & The Crickets music on a secondary school trip to Melrose, in the Scottish Borders and I loved the music I heard. A few years passed before I heard it again, and it blew me away. I then remembered my old acoustic guitar was in the loft (attic), which my parents bought for me as a Christmas present many years before. I brought that old acoustic guitar down, put some fishing gut on it to use for strings (couldn't afford strings), and I taught myself to play guitar by taping Buddy Holly & The Crickets songs from the radio. I played the songs over and over as I learnt to play guitar. I learnt to play one string at a time listening to Peggy Sue, Oh Boy, Maybe Baby etc....and as I learnt to play, I added more stings into the chords I learned from those songs.

After 2-3 years of practice, I was invited to join a local Rock Band as a lead guitarist. Since then, I have been in umpteen bands over a 12 year period, playing Rock, Pop, Indie, Metal/Grunge, Country Rock, just about anything guitar based. I played on the local live circuit for 10 years or so. I ended up fronting my own three piece combos towards the end of that period, playing live in and around my hometown of Glasgow.

So to say the least, Buddy Holly & The Crickets have been monumental in my music career. What I know about music, songwriting, singing, recording etc all comes from a bunch of guys who loved what they done.

The music of Buddy Holly & The Crickets is genuine, honest, heartfelt yet passionate and I firmly believe bands and musicians will still be using Buddy Holly & The Crickets songs as a reference of quality for many years to come.

Pete Carroll (2009)

When and how did you discover the music?

'The Music'/Rock n Roll seemed to arrive from nowhere on the radio in the UK mid-50s, era of (Coral star) Teresa Brewer's jaunty 'Music Music Music' and Guy Mitchell & Frankie Laine big ballads, though I recall being intrigued by the lyrics of Kay Starr's 'Rock n Roll Waltz' and being impressed with Tennessee Ernie Ford's country-rock tale of worker exploitation '16 Tons'. Then at a wedding-reception in 1956 'Rock Around The Clock' with my older cousins jiving flat-out to the record repeatedly played. I recall becoming really Elvis-aware while on holiday in Norfolk in '57 .Then by late '57 our family had a Grundig reel-to-reel tape recorder and my younger brother and I would tape the BBC Top-20 from the sheet-music charts aired late every Sunday evening by Pete Murray. I distinctly recall rushing home from some outing just in time to hear-and-tape the Top-5 which included the rebel-rousing 'Oh, Boy'.

Though I didn't then know that Buddy was lead writer/guitarist/singer of The Crickets. 'That'll Be The Day' and 'Maybe Baby' soon afterwards made their marks on me, in that order, also being sung, hummed and whistled in and out of school and everywhere else. Somehow I missed out on 'Peggy Sue' until later and then, WOW! My first realisation of 'Buddy Holly' was when Canadian D.J. & actor, who still acts in theatre & TV, Trevor Peacock in his authentic north-American twang back-announced on Radio Luxembourg in the summer of '58 "That was 'Burrdy Haally with, Rrrave Ohn !" Having seen no photo of Buddy that I can recall, for some reason I imagined a country-mountain cowboy in jeans and check-shirt. I was deeply impressed by Trevor's delivery and Buddy's blast !!

Were you a Buddy Holly fan?

As above, (before his early death which brought a whole new perspective still panning-out), no more than a fan of virtually every other new young U.S. Rockers of that classic opening era. Most young Brits then knew that UK cover-versions and clones were just craven, crap-copies - including later The Beatles & Stones, trying to out-Berry Chuck Berry and the original black super-Rockers because none of us could write or perform our own real Rock n Roll!! Except for the tragically understated Ian 'Sammy' Samwell-Smith from Cheshunt, who wrote 'Move It' and other greats for Cliff and was then cruelly dropped when Cliff & The Shads sold-out to mainstream 'Pop'.

Were you a Ritchie Valens fan?

Yep, particularly 'La Bamba' & 'Bluebirds Over The Mountain' plus 'Donna'. Well again did 17 year old Ritchie make a bad cut?

Were you a Big Bopper fan?

Everyone immediately lurved 'Chantilly Lace'. I later I noticed his writer credits on east-Texan Johnny Preston's big-hit 'Running Bear' , with music-press info that White Dove. was the name of a soap-block popular with women which Jape had made into 'little White Dove'.

J.P. Richardson another versatile super-talent and gone at 29.

There are only two times I remember Cecil mentioning his brother. The first time, I had gone into his office for who knows what reason, turn in paperwork, etc. And I said, "Hey Cecil, I heard (from the other hands) the Big Bopper was your brother. Is that true? (or something very close to that.) He kinda smiled and said, "Yeah, he was ". I felt a little awkward talking to him about his brother since we were not close friends and all I could think of to say was, "I really liked Chantilly Lace ". He smiled again and said, "Yeah, it was a good song. Thanks. "

The other time was when Chester and I went to his house. We were in the living room. I nodded toward a picture on the wall and said, "Is that your brother ?" He looked and said, "Yeah, that's Jay." (Oddly enough, up until that moment the only name I knew his brother by was "The Big Bopper ", although I was smart enough to have figured out by that time that his last name was Richardson). So now I knew him as Jay Richardson. Hey. I figured it all out later.

Buddy was my favorite later, after I had started listening to rock 'n roll. My older brother Jimmy introduced me to Buddy Holly because his favorite song was "Rave On ". Mine was "Maybe Baby ". And that would have been around 62 or 63.

I have truly regretted that I never just sat down with Cecil and talked to him about Jay. I would have liked to have known all about him, too. Chances like that don't come often in life.

Rikko (2008)

I discovered 1950's music in general via my older brother's and parents record collection. I came along much later than my siblings and was thoroughly engaged by artists such as Little Richard, Buddy Holly, Chuck Berry, Fats Domino, Jerry Lee Lewis, Gene Vincent, Elvis and the Everly Brothers. I remember my friends at the time proclaiming that this kind of music was "old fashioned" but I strongly disagreed. I just couldn't get into late 70's disco. I like music where you can hear the lyrics and rock to the beat. These artists from that era had incredible talent and artistry and ability to simply go into a studio and knock out a live recording without overdubbing or all the pitch correction that they do these days. The music has lived on thru new generations simply because it's great. It's also before rock music became political or had a "message" to it. This was fun, happy music and everyone likes that. Buddy Holly specifically will shine on as he forever represents the innocent next door neighbor that becomes a rock and roll star, giving hope to kids everywhere that you don't have to look like Elvis to get people to listen to you. Pure genius.

John Mueller

I've been a fan of the guy and his music since 1958. Even though I'd heard those great songs in '57, I wasn't yet interested in music. Guess it took turning 13 early in '58 to wake me up.

Yes, I do remember reading the story in both the Baltimore News-Post and the Baltimore Evening Sun when I got home from high school on February 3, 1959. I had no idea the crash had occurred until I saw the papers. I don't remember any mention on TV or radio here back then.

We still played all three guys' records at the teen center and CYO dances anyway, at least until I reached age 18 in 1963 and couldn't go to those dances anymore.

Here we are, over 40 years later, and that music still sounds like it was just recorded yesterday.

Jack Miller (2009)

"I remember the time...
I attended Lubbock High School for all three years of my high school days. I knew who Buddy Holly, J.I. Allison, Niki Sullivan, Bob Montgomery, Echo McGuire and several other people associated with Buddy Holly were. Since LHS was the only white high school in Lubbock until the Fall of 1955, all the white students in town were at our school, which had about 2,200 students. I remember seeing Buddy Holly in the choir. J.I. (Jerry then) Allison was in a class with me. I remember seeing Buddy, Bob and Larry perform in a program at the "Westerner Days" activities. We were the Lubbock High "Westerners" and one day a year we dressed in western clothes and hats and remembered our heritage on the South Plains of Texas. Lubbock County was only 64 years old when we graduated from high school. Buddy in his jeans and western/bluegrass music fit right in with the celebration of "Westerner Days". Being isolated from a lot of the rest of the state of Texas because of our location, the kids in '55 occupied their time with music. They enjoyed hearing the music on the radio and TV but liked making their own "live" music.

One day, my boyfriend (a student at Texas Tech University and later my husband and a backup singer for Buddy and The Crickets), John Pickering, invited me to go with him to the Pontiac car dealership showroom where Elvis Presley was performing before a big show that night at the Fair Park Coliseum. Buddy Holly was also in the crowd at the dealership.
Each week all the students would gather in the auditorium for assemblies of programs and entertainment and I would see Buddy and all the others involved in the music there as well as in the halls between classes and in classes. Of course at that time he was not famous and The Crickets had not been formed. Our football team was very successful in those days and many of us would be seen at the football games that were held at the college stadium because of the big attendance by the city.

My memories continue with the recordings John, his brother Bill and friend Bob Lapham did in the summer of 1957 and October of 1957. They did the backup vocals on 9 of the 12 songs on the only group-sound album that would be recorded and released while Buddy Holly was alive, "The Chirping Crickets" 1957 album.

Vicky Billington Pickering

I had lived in Lubbock various times through the years and had moved back there in 1952 to attend Texas Tech University. From 1952 to 1955, I remember going from Texas Tech to Lubbock High School to perform at assemblies and would see and hear Buddy and his group performing during some of those years. I had known Buddy and the Holley family for many years when they would come to see my family, The Pickering Family Quartet, perform in the Lubbock area. We were radio singers there.

I heard of Buddy and his friends and his girlfriend, Echo through my girlfriend and future wife, Vicky Billington. She was in the 1955 class with Buddy and several of the other musicians. In the summer of 1957, my brother Bill and friend Bob Lapham did recordings for Norman Petty at his 7th Street Recording Studio in Clovis, NM. We saw Buddy and the then Crickets and saw them working in the studio. We were honored to be asked to put backup vocals on 9 songs that were included on the only group-sound album that was released while Buddy Holly was alive, "The Chirping Crickets" album.

We finished our work on the album in October. It was released November 27, 1957. In December, we saw Buddy in Lubbock and he jumped out of his car in downtown Lubbock and came to where Bill and I were standing on the sidewalk and told us "Thanks for the work you did on the songs. You guys made the album." I had married and moved to Corpus Christi, Texas and gone to work as a petroleum geologist and then spent 6 months in Virginia and Fort Hood Texas in the military in 1958 so I did not see Buddy again. I watched him from afar until the plane crash and am still amazed that now, 52 years later, his songs are still playing on the radio and almost everyone I have ever met knew who Buddy Holly was.

John Pickering, The Picks

I met Buddy in 1953 when we were sophomores in high school and were friends for the next six years; you mentioned the duo of Buddy and Bob. I was a fan of Bob's more than Buddy because Bob's style of singing was more to my liking. I was a friend to Buddy outside of his music. What most people don't know is that Buddy was a pretty fair electrician if memory serves me. Buddy worked as an appliance repair man for Minter's fixit shop which was across the street from LHS. I think they may still be in business there. Buddy and I were members of a vocation club called the V. I. C. club in the fall of 1953 the auto mechanics class cut a Ford engine in two. Buddy built an electric eye and when you covered the eye with your hand it would activate an electric motor hooked to the engine and the motor would turn over just as if it was running a car. We displayed it at the South Plains fair and Buddy and I teamed up to man the booth one night. I wonder how many people remember that.

The last time I saw Buddy was in the middle of 1958. Me, Don Pendergrass, and Jimmy Rinehart was at the Hi-Di-Ho Jnr on Fourth and College and Buddy came up. W spent about an hour with him. He talked about his upcoming marriage and about the tour he was fixing to go on. Also he said he was in negotiation with Ed Sullivan to appear on his television show again. I never saw Buddy after that night.

I thank you for asking me about Buddy as he was a friend.

John (Sonny) Dunn

The Bopper

There's one guy I won't forget,
He had a special way of spinning discs,
He was a legend he was a star
on the radio by far.

'Hello Baby' that's what he'd say,
At the start of Chantilly Lace.
His trademark signature I can't ignore,
It's the Big Bopper who I adore.

A great performer who stole the show
On TV, STAGE and RADIO.
Across the country through out the land
You sang your songs with your touring band.

He was a legend, he was a star,
It's the Big Bopper that I adore.

Words by Jason Seymour (2009)

BUDDY HOLLY AND THE CRICKETS

PERFORMING IN LONDON ON THE

SUNDAY NIGHT AT THE LONDON

PALLADIUM T/V SHOW

MARCH 2 1958

PHOTO BY TOM GIBSON OF BRENTFORD UK.

PHOTO BY TOM GIBSON OF BRENTFORD UK.

I was the only Buddy Holly fan, and main rock 'n' roll fan, in my house. I was 14 years old in 1958.
My mum liked some of it. She did like Elvis but definitely not Buddy! When I asked her why, she would only say she didn't like his voice.
My younger sister didn't seem to be very interested in any of it - she was 11 in 1958. My dad had no time for it at all, and thought it was all just a disgusting noise!!

The photo'??

Well, during the Sunday afternoon of the show - the programme aired at 8.00 pm - I suddenly wondered whether my dad could take a photo' of Holly from the t/v. Just how or why I came up with the idea I don't know.

My father was a keen amateur photographer. He always carried his camera with him when we went for days out, and he liked to take portraits of us at home, so he had a tripod. He also developed and printed his own films.

I asked him about taking a photo'. I don't think that he had ever thought of doing something like that, so the idea intrigued him.

He did go and look through some photography magazines, and told me that it was not an easy thing to do, but he would have a go.

In those days the t/v picture was made up of something like 500 lines, which were always moving and changing. So, to get a photo', the camera would have to be set at a fast speed, one would think!!

But, the t/v screen was actually not that bright, so that meant a slower speed was necessary. My memory is that my dad set the camera up on his tripod, and set the speed at 1/30 sec. He took only two photos - one that I sent you, and one of the whole group, which did not come out very well at all. (I will dig it out and send a copy.)

He had a good eye for it because there is a photo', taken from the t/v by a professional photographer, that must have been taken within milliseconds of my dad's photo'. The only difference is the professional's photo' is a sharper and clearer, especially around the lips. (Don't worry about using the photo' I sent you. It is my dad's - I have the negative.) Anyway, I'm very grateful to my dad for taking that photo'.

As I've said, my father had absolutely no interest in Buddy and his music, or his performance!!

So, maybe I should tell you my recollections of the show?
I was very excited when the show started.

Buddy and the Crickets were the first act on.
(They had to leave straight after their performance for another show on their UK tour.)
I don't remember what they sang, although I do now have the three songs on bootleg CDs. I was a little disappointed that there were no backing vocals - for about 20 seconds!! Buddy's strong vocals soon made me forget about them!!

But, Buddy did seem nervous.

He did not say anything between songs, which did disappoint me. And that is about it!!
There is just one strange thing, that I do remember, that happened after Buddy's performance.

The Palladium theatre stage is quite big, and the curtains that close across the stage are large and heavy. They are opened and closed, between acts, by a water-powered hydraulic system. (I learnt this some years later.)

Something happened on the show that night that had never happened before and never happened again - well, certainly never during the broadcasting of this show.
After Buddy's performance, the curtains would not close.

So the compere of the show - Robert Morley, an actor -, who would normally come out in front of the curtains, as the artists left the stage behind the curtains, came out and apologised for the failure of the curtains to close.

Buddy could be seen walking off behind him.

I have always clearly remembered that. All I can say is - strange!!

Peter Gibson, Harrow, UK

Earl Sinks, Jerry Allison, Sonny Curtis and Joe B Mauldin.

Lubbock circa late 1958 / early 1959.

This story was told to me by Bo Roberts.

Bo Roberts was a young inspiring musician and songwriter from Amarillo, Texas. I got to know Bo through my trips back and forth to the Florabama during the Frank Brown Songwriters Festival. He would tell me dirty jokes and stories about growing up in Lubbock in the time of Buddy and The Crickets. Turns out that Bo knew Earl. He constantly followed Earl around, back when Earl first started on Dot Records with a release of "I Am The Man".

Bo said "I remember going down to the soda shop in Lubbock where Earl's record was on the juke box. I wore that record out playing it so much and waiting for him to come in the shop like he did almost every day.

At that time Earl was seeing a girl that worked there. Anyhow I would always ask about going with him to see the others. The others being J.I. Allison, Joe B. Mauldin.

Over at Henry Earl's house all the guys were rehearsing. And that was the day. A day I will never forget. He introduced me to Buddy. I thought I was going to shit myself. Well they never would let me join in. But I didn't care. I would stick around till afterward so Earl could teach me a few chords. I would run home and practice all week until the next time.

He never did seem to want to see what I learned but that was alright with me, another two or three chords the next time. I would watch Buddy and the guys practice then Earl would take time to teach me more. I may not have become a writer if it was not for Earl introducing me to Buddy Holly and the Crickets".

Later on Bo went on to write songs such as "You're Out Doing What I'm Here Doing Without" by Gene Watson, also "Ten With A Two" by Willie Nelson, and many more.

Just from a 45 single on Dot Records of Earl Sinks singing his song "I Am The Man", and taking time for a little red-headed kid with a guitar and a dream who was willing to learn to play after getting to meet Buddy Holly and The Crickets through Earl Sinks, came forth another of 'Texas' own sons that became a great singer-songwriter

Brandon Sinks

I remember working with all three and they were all great guys and performers.

Because the Chantels were very sheltered we weren't allowed to hang out with the guy groups we traveled and did shows with. We were after all ages 13-17. In those days we traveled with a chaperone and our manager who were very protective

We were allowed to watch shows from the wings of the theatres where we performed and were able to tell the performers that we enjoyed their show. Then for us it was back up to the dressing room to do homework or just sit and wait for the next show or if it was one show we would wait for the finale.

Lois Harris Powell (The Chantels)

My dad Teddy Drake was a songwriter who also played guitar and sang songs he wrote. He was very active with Phil Everly of The Everly Brothers. One day he was with Phil Everly and my dad asked Phil to call me to surprise me on the phone. Phil called me and I was so happy that I could finally tell my girlfriends that I talked to Phil Everly on the phone. Well no one would believe me that I talked to Phil Everly.

Time went by and Buddy and Maria came to Torrance to visit the family. Buddy was a Phil and Don fan. He wanted to meet them so my dad invited Phil and Don to come to Torrance to meet Buddy.

Well only Phil came. I got my picture taken that day with Phil on my parents' fireplace seat in our living room to prove that Phil was at my house.

Buddy, Teddy, and Phil all got together and had a jam session that day. I was so excited to hear them. They all had guitars and great voices. That trio was the best I had ever heard!

Donna Burgess (Donna Drake) 2010

Musical Dreams of John Pickering

In the past couple of years I've had musical dreams about departed family members and friends. I don't dream often, and when I do, these dreams I've been having are positive and uplifting. I awake happy and sometimes in the middle of a song which, when suddenly awake, I continue to sing softly.

In dreams, I have done stage appearances with my departed mom (Beth), dad (John M), and my only sibling, my older brother Bill, known as The Pickering Family Quartet. Sometimes we sing onstage together in concert before large audiences, just like we did so often in the 1940s and early 1950s. I participate, and I hear and feel the close harmony just like I did so many times in the past. Dad sings and plays his guitar accompaniment, and we alternate solo parts and backup singing. Our last full-family radio show was on the morning of March 13, 1953. Dad died a few hours later at age 52. The fact that I'm the only one still living this life doesn't enter into it. If I could, I would dial up such dreams often, but I can't make it happen. They are rare dreams, and I'm not in charge.

I've occasionally dreamed of visiting with my father who has been gone for many years but my late brother Bill has visited me only twice. He never stays long, just like in real life. Always anxious to get away.

I've recently dreamed of Norman Petty playing a new song he'd just written for me to hear. He played it from a lead sheet at the piano. This was strange because Norman didn't read music. It was a beautiful song and when he asked, I told him so. But when I awoke I couldn't remember the tune.

A couple of nights ago (March 20, 2010), for the first time ever I had a dream about Buddy Holly. In it I found myself standing only a few feet, from where he was sitting on a stool. I didn't walk up to where I was standing – I was just suddenly there. There were other people standing around, and it appeared to be outdoors. It seemed that we were summoned to him; not the other way around. I didn't recognize any of the others, nor did I try to.
Buddy was accepting a music sheet from a girl who looked to be in her twenties. He turned to me and said, "Hello". I nodded to him, and he smiled. He told me, "I'm looking for songs, John, and I've just accepted one from her." He nodded to the girl.
I replied, "Well, I didn't come prepared, Buddy. I don't want to try to replace her song, but I've got a lot of them at home."
It seemed that everyone there, male and female, were songwriters, but none of them said a word as Buddy and I spoke.
For some reason, an unpublished song that I wrote years ago came to me, and I said, "Buddy, I can sing you one." He said, "Go ahead"

So, in my dream I sang him a song called, "Not With Your Heart". Everyone there was listening as I explained the song.

I told Buddy that it's about a boyfriend that's caught his girlfriend cheating, and you can tell that he's upset with her. Then I sang:

"You've been telling me 'love'
Only with your eyes,
You've been saying that you love me, baby,
Then goin' out and doin' otherwise.
You've been acting so innocent,
While you play the other part,
You've been telling me 'love' with your eyes and your lips,
Not with your heart!
I've got to tell you, baby,
Why do you desire to roam?
Why go flocking with the sparrows, girl,
With a 'bird of paradise' at home?
Now you tell me you're finished,
Girl you never did start,
You've been telling me love with your eyes and your lips,
 Not with your heart!"

© John Pickering Music Co. "Not With Your Heart"

Buddy smiled, nodded and said, "John, let's get together when I'm finished here."

At that instant, in my dream I silently rose up from the scene and found myself looking down from above at our conversation. There was only silence. I saw both of us and I could see that we were talking and gesturing with our hands. None of the others in the group moved at all. They faded in my view. We appeared congenial, but I couldn't hear what we were saying.

I saw that Buddy looked about 22 years old, but different. His hair was medium brown and not black and slicked back Not only did he not wear black horned rim glasses, he wore none at all. He looked happy, and I was glad.
I then saw myself my hair was dark brown, not white as it is now. I didn't have glasses on, either, and I looked as I did in my early 20s.
I woke up feeling good. I always do from musical dreams. They come more often now, and I've wondered why. The meaning escapes me, but I've searched for meaning. My search has led me to a Bible passage in Joel 2:28 about the Spirit of God, which is repeated in Acts 2:17. Written in each passage are words which include, "Your young men shall see visions, and your old men shall dream dreams."

In the fifties flying saucers were in vogue. If one had landed outside the BBC in London to deliver the next No.1 hit it could not have sounded stranger than 'That'll Be The Day' by The Crickets. It sliced like a three bladed knife through the suffocating big band pap that dominated the ether on the Light Programme. Everything about it was loose, lascivious and different. We hadn't even seen an electric guitar in '57, let alone a Fender Stratocaster which rang out so clear. And those backing singers sounded like a chorus of harpies, taking a day off a horror movie film set. But most of all there was the lead vocal coming on like a demented cross between Little Richard and Frankie Lymon - so of course he had to be black as well as young and totally weird.

Having not discovered the music press, the sparse information on the 78 rpm disc was all we had to go on. The stark black Vogue-Coral label came in the most functional and basic brown paper sleeve. It seemed that the record moguls were deliberately trying to preserve the mystery of this group. Then Pete Murray announced on TV's '6.5 Special' jukebox spot that Buddy Holly was the singer's name and played 'Peggy Sue' for us. Crazy name - and an even wackier but still wonderful record. Finally in February 1958 the Daily Mirror announced that Buddy was coming to Britain and for the first time I saw the tousled dark hair and those horn rims. The complexion was amazingly white and the expression inscrutable yet knowing. I still believe that John Lennon followed this example on the cover of 'A Hard Day's Night'.

Live appearances by American rock n rollers were still a huge novelty in England. And given that alongside Elvis and Little Richard, Buddy was the biggest idol on our gang's hit parade. His imminent arrival seemed like a combination of ET landing and a youthful god coming down from Olympus. Given that many pubescent nascent rock n roll fans felt the same, it is hard to recapture the anticipation and thrill so many felt when Buddy and the guys played live on national TV that Sunday night in March 1958. OK I'm a sexagenarian now but on the inside I'm still the same age as my shirt size (that's 16.5 in England!)

Barry Holley - Yorkshire, England.

I first heard songs by The Crickets as long ago as 1957/1958 when I was in school and to me they stood out from all the other wonderful Rock 'n' Roll music of that era.

I also liked Elvis, Ricky Nelson and The Everly Brothers to name but 3 but somehow the sound of The Crickets appealed to me more than the others.

It was only later I discovered that the lead singer was Buddy Holly and that he also had records out with a similar sound which I liked. Of course now I realise they were one and the same. The first song I heard was 'That'll Be The Day', which I heard from someone's portable radio and it kind of hit me like one of those defining moments in your life when you heard or found out something for the first time. Maybe the first time you were in love !! I got to the stage where I would buy the new Crickets or Buddy record without even listening to them and I was never disappointed, well maybe a bit with 'Early In The Morning' / ' Now Were One' !

Then came the plane crash and like Don MacLean I really did see it on the front page of the newspapers for the first time, while out delivering.

I liked the musical simplicity, the wonderful tunes and the sound. It had and still has a feel to it that I do not get from other artists of that era. Listen today to old stuff from The Norman Petty studio and you can hear how dated it sounds, but not any of the Buddy Holly stuff.

He was not just from that era but from every era.

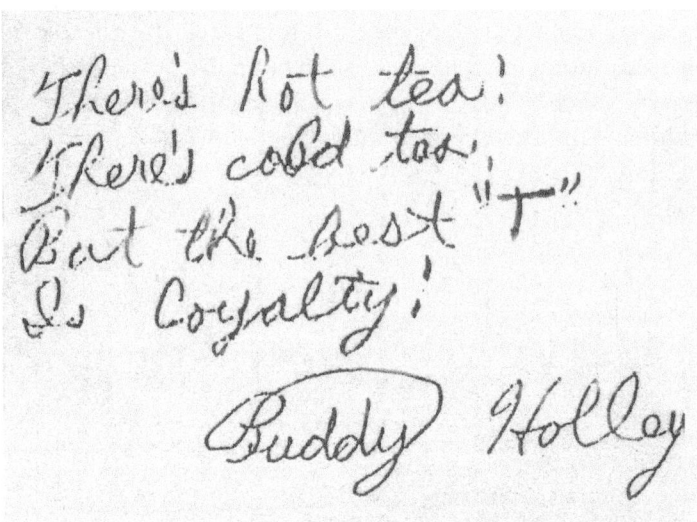

This was given to me by 'Big Ed' Wilkes at radio station KDAV, Lubbock, Texas.
'Big Ed' was the driving force behind this radio station. The original copy is in his wife's autograph book which she had when she was a teenager. He told me that Buddy Holly had written this poem in her book on the school bus on the way to Lubbock High School.

Tony Warran - London

At 17 years old Ritchie Valens was already one of the most electrifying guitarists around and he was just beginning to blossom as a songwriter.

He was only 17 !! He was a true blue Rock and Roller and the world of rock and roll missed out on a real gem because of one decision he made in 1959 and a simple twist of fate with the flip of a coin. 'Come On Let's Go' is one of my favorite rock and roll songs of all time. Its pure 50s, its pure Valens and in a little more than 2 minutes, it makes the case that we lost a real rock and roll hero in 1959- someone who was just starting to show the world what he was made of. Just like Buddy Holly .

Seven Garabedian

It's the love of the music that those three entertainers gave us that binds us, one Holly fan to another, even total strangers become life-long friends, that's the STRENGHTH OF THE MUSIC

Gary Clevenger

When I picked up my brother's guitar at around 12 years old I would listen and play by ear the early Beatle songs. I thought they were the best until my brother played 'Rave On' for me. I asked him who wrote that and he said Buddy Holly and by the way he is a Lubbock native. From that time on I listened to the music and studied his song writing. By the way a lot of his songs have that chugging beat like an old locomotive. 'That'll be the day' really gives a hint of a train moving down the track. You feel the beat of his rhythm on guitar and percussion and his 'whoo-hoo' which reminds me of the whistle. What an amazing song writer. He was so far ahead of his time and today.

J Rodmar (2009)

I know for a fact that if I had a choice I would choose to have grown up in the 1950s, along with the new sound of rock and roll and the innocence of those times, jukeboxes, malt shops and drive-inns.

Sevan Garabedian

I discovered the music whilst running a youth club and also teaching members to play musical instruments and forming groups. In those early days we used to listen to a pirate radio station / Radio Luxembourg, which faded in and out.

Kenneth Coombes

Buddy Holly's music still resonates today because of the quality of the songs and the talented musicians that he worked with. And because I discovered the music much later, I was able to see how he influenced so many musicians who came after him particularly The Beatles and The Rolling Stones

Joe Beine

A time where people were kinder to one another and there wasn't so much fear and mistrust in the world. After what happened on February 3 1959, there was a shift and although it didn't directly affect what happened in the next decade and the decades to come, symbolically it was the end of an era. Of that there is no question.

Sevan Garabedian

I have made hundreds of friends from all over the world, Europe, South Africa, Australia as well as the USA, and my native England, all because of a plane crash in Iowa 1959, and the love of the music.
It joins people from all walks of life from Scotland Yard detectives to insurance salesman, printers to architects, all with one passion.

Clive Harvey

I started performing as the Big Bopper over ten years ago. Tried singing Chantilly Lace at a Karaoke night and all of a sudden people started to applaud so it went on from there. I've always seen myself as a performer and I love the whole essence of the 50s, the music, the clothes, and for the first time teenagers could express themselves.
I wanted to do a tribute act and I searched for a character that was the opposite of me. I am quite a shy person and I needed a character that took me away from myself, hence The Big Bopper, Jiles Perry Richardson was a man very much like myself offstage, he was shy and unassuming but on stage he was big, and he was bold, he was an extrovert.
The Bopper suited me and I suited him.

Martyn Gille

I was first introduced to Buddy's music at about 8 yrs of age when I came across an album that my older sisters had. After leaving school I was reintroduced to his music when I began to gain an interest in Rock N Roll and Rockabilly Music. Buddy quickly became my favorite even above the likes of Elvis. Having formed a band with some friends, I of course insisted that we perform some Holly material in the set. People began to comment on how much I sounded like him and when I added the glasses (just for fun really) how much I looked like him. It all snowballed from there until we found ourselves performing a complete tribute to him and the Crickets. We were one of the 1st Tribute bands around forming not long after the Bootleg Beatles. Hence the name Bootleg Buddy. The band eventually split up and I formed my own band The Counterfeit Crickets.

Marcus Robinson

I was a private pilot late in life for about 15 years. Nothing is more frightening than for a non-instrument pilot getting trapped in clouds. I came close a time or two. You have zero chance of survival if you are without visual reference for forty seconds. Zero.
I'm sure Roger was a young man who when presented the opportunity of paling around with the young stars, particularly Buddy, he couldn't resist. It probably was a clear night when he committed and like many another scud-running pilot he rationalized into thinking he could make it.
One wonders what this young man's life would've been like, had he said "Sorry, guys. I can't fly instrument yet. I'm close in my lessons, but not there. Guess you'll have to hop on the bus".

If only he had!

Bob Lapham

I do remember the only time I ever saw the Crickets perform was in Odessa. They were on tour as an opening act for country music star Faron Young.

I really didn't know them then and am not too sure as to who was accompanying him.

I suspect it was Jerry Allison and Don Guess. It should be in Bill Griggs' "Day by Day". It was probably early in the summer of 1957. I'd never heard of Buddy Holly or the Crickets.

My family didn't have a record player; hence, we never bought any records. At any rate, they had Buddy and the boys perform down on the "track" of the football stadium and had a huge platform stage for the "stars". They didn't even let Buddy up on that big "Faron Young" stage. I also remember him singing "Blue Day/Black Nights", "Brown Eyed Handsome Man", and then he said, "I'd like to sing one song made popular by one of your local favorites, then he sang "Ooby Dooby".

When he came to Odessa to recruit Tommy and Carl for the Winter Dance Party, I was home from college for the holiday season. I don't remember if it was Thanksgiving or Christmas. Probably Thanksgiving. Bill's books should also have that date. Anyway I called Ronnie Smith who had been my vocalist in the Poor Boys and now trying to make it alone. He asked me if I wanted to go to the Silver Saddle Club, a local dive in which Tommy and his Western swing band were playing. There was almost no one there.

If memory serves me, and again no one suggested I take notes and it's been well over 50 years, I think Buddy and Waylon were there sitting at a table with Tommy, Ronnie and me. Carl was not there although they were discussing the possibility of his joining the Winter Dance Party.

I remember a little later, Jerry (we never called him J. I. back then), Peggy Sue, Joe B., Buddy Knox and his new bride came through Odessa and called Ronnie. This was probably during the Christmas holiday time and I was also back home from college. They came by Ronnie's house and we all sat up most of the night just talking. They were talking about not wanting to be up north during the harsh winter and about not wanting to live in New York City for their professional careers. They preferred to be in West Texas.

Another good Roy story. I think this was during Christmas of 1959. Roy and Ronnie Smith (sans Poor Boys) were contracted to play a dance at the youth center in Ruidoso, NM. A friend of mine from Odessa and I decided to take a road trip up there. We went to the youth center and thought the event had been canceled. Roy and Ronnie played the entire dance with only two couples there. I felt very sorry for them. A few months later, Roy released "Only the Lonely".

When Roy and the Teen Kings would go on a road tour, my band the Poor Boys would do their live weekly television show on KOSA-TV in Odessa sponsored by Pioneer Furniture. There was no videotape at the time so none exists of any of the shows. I'd give anything to have one. There is no fear like doing live TV.

I discovered it about the same time Buddy did. Before R&R or Rockabilly, we all did Country Music....the music of Hank Williams, Lefty Frizzell, Ernest Tubb and Eddy Arnold. Johnny Cash was coming in at the time. When Elvis hit the charts and the road, we all traded in the steel guitars and fiddles for Strats and drums. We still favored the upright bass fiddles, ala Bill Black. We did adopt the 4-5 piece band of a lead and rhythm guitar, drums and bass, Sometimes the vocalists could play the guitar, sometimes he couldn't, I remember Roy Orbison, who was living and playing in Odessa at the time, had an electric mandolin left over from the "country" days. He didn't have to fire the player. They fired him. True story. The Teen Kings fired Orbison!

We never had an idea of what was to come 50 years down the road or I would have taken notes. I saw him perform only once but did meet him another time when he was in Odessa to hire Tommy Allsup for the WDP and also hire my drummer, Carl Bunch. My band,, the Poor Boys, didn't do a lot of Buddy's music, our lead vocalist was into Elvis. We broke up in the summer of '58.

We liked Ritchie but didn't do his music. Carl and Ritchie were close friends on the WDP as they were the two "kids" on the bus.

I'm just amazed that it lasted so long. Also I am amazed that people attend festivals honoring those pioneers who came and went during my lifetime. I've also sure enjoyed maintaining the old friendships like Peggy Sue and Tommy Allsup and making the new ones like Gary and Ramona, The Pickerings and the Fireballs. I too enjoy the music festivals and the museums.

I've told this story before but in case you haven't heard it, The Poor Boys were playing a sock hop in Odessa and during the break we were in the back on a smoke break. There was a bang on the stage door. We answered it and there stood Roy Orbison, alone, wanting to come in the back door so he wouldn't have to pay the half buck we were charging to come in the front door. We made $300 that night. That was $60 each for the five band members. I never took a larger portion than anyone else received.

Richard Porter (2009)

Lubbock 1980

Arrived in Lubbock on the evening of Sept. 2 after a long, bor-r-ing bus ride from Tacoma. After a bath and something to eat I spent the rest of the evening talking with Buddy Holly fans that were already there. Mary Ann Prashina of Indiana and I decided to share a room to save on expenses. This worked out well since she had a video camera and I got to watch "instant replays" of things like the statue unveiling and the concerts of the Lubbock group, 'The Echoes of Holly'.

There were not as many window displays as I had expected but some of them were very good. It was easy to spot Don Larson's room by the turkeys on the door. The Ding-a-Ling Clones (Barb Rau & Penny Sue Falker) had to room next to the Larson's as was evident by the signs on their window, courtesy of Don Larson. Bill Griggs had the room next to Barb and Penny Sue.

Also I finally got to meet Gaatse Zoodsma of Holland with whom I had been corresponding for 7 years. He was a bit smaller that I expected (I'm taller than he is) but great fun to be with. He photographed everything as he is a camera nut but this is probably his only chance to come to Lubbock. He is quite a good photographer. When he wasn't taking pictures, he was swimming or telling dumb jokes. We had a more than sufficient supply of people prone to telling dumb jokes; this sometimes included Susie (me).
After a few hastily grabbed hours of something remotely resembling sleep we were up early and were able to procure copies of the Lubbock paper to check for articles about Buddy.

On Wed., Sept. 3, Mary Ann Prashina (and video camera), her boy friend, Ed Liss , Gaatse and I set out on our own private tour of Lubbock. Main objective – postcards of Lubbock, which are difficult to find. Ed had a couple of addresses where he'd heard that they were available (and then probably of Texas Tech). But first we went to the City of Lubbock Cemetery to say hello to Buddy. There was one small bouquet of flowers on his grave. After saying our private greetings to our mutual idol and hero we went looking for postcards at a downtown address which turned out to be the bus station (which looks nothing at all like the one in the movie). So we took pictures and nearly cleaned out their supply of the few postcards available of Lubbock. Gaatse must have bought most of the postcards for sale in the entire city. Lubbock is the hardest city I know of to find picture postcards in. Then we tootled off to some shopping center and located more cards in a drug store. They didn't have many when we left. Then we located a gift shop in the same mall and while they didn't have postcards, they had souvenirs. Gaatse couldn't resist buying a Texas "fly swatter" (over a yard long) and the matching fly (9" long). Then it was over to U. V. Blake's record store where Suzie found the Holly House album by Larry and Travis Holley and was unable to resist temptation. I bought it even though Larry was due at the hotel the next day to sell it for less.

So, hot, tired, package-laden, and considerably less solvent, we went back to the Villa Inn and found out that we'd just missed the local TV news crew. For the rest of the day we visited and talked with the others and that evening we listened to an impromptu concert by a Lubbock performer, Joey Allen doing Buddy Holly songs and other tunes of the 50's. He's very good.

Next day, Thur., Sept. 4, was the first day of the planned activity. So after breakfast, Nick Rossi of New York and I went to the little shopping center across the street from the hotel, looking for flowers for Buddy. The grocery store had none but the dime store further down the mall had a lovely array of artificial bouquets and dried arrangements. It was difficult to choose. Nick bought a lovely wreath of yellow roses, and I got a round wreath of similar roses for the bouquet that Win Hannenberg of Holland had requested that I buy and place on the grave for him.

Also got a bouquet of white roses backed by orange and blue dried arrangements for my birthday present to Buddy. Then we went back to the hotel, and after showing the flowers to other people and telling them where we got them, I went up to my room and affixed cards to the bouquets (I had prepared a special birthday card for Bud).

At noon most of the Holly fans at the hotel left on a chartered city bus on the scheduled tour of Lubbock. There was insufficient time to visit every place in Lubbock with Holly significance. But we visited Mr. & Mrs. Holley's house (outside only), the birthplace (a vacant lot now), a house where Joe B. lived in 1958, Hutchinson Jr. High, Lubbock High School (inside and out and where some of the students were filming us), the roller rink where Buddy often played in his early days (no, it doesn't have a neon half moon on top [like in the beginning of "The Buddy Holly Story" movie]), and finally the cemetery. Nick and I set out the bouquets for Buddy .Most of the fans were waiting for the memorial service to put flowers on the grave, but I had promised Buddy last time to give him flowers as soon as possible this time, the white roses that have a very intense, personal meaning to me. We all had our own private devotions at the graveside.

During all of our tour, we were accompanied by a black station wagon belonging to the news crew of channel 28.

After returning to the hotel, it was display-buy-sell time. After setting up my display of photos of my Holly collection, I made the rounds of the other tables to see what goodies were on sale. Lots and lots of goodies, far more than my limited budget could afford. Photos, records, sheet music, buttons, books. Larry and Travis Holley arrived during this period and were selling their LP [Holly's House] and autographing copies of it and the superb booklet on Buddy that it contains. I got so many Holly lapel buttons that I had to buy a Holly cap from Don Larson in order to display them.

Larry Matti and the rest of the Green Bay [Wisconsin] gang had finally arrived and their display of the Feb. 1, 59 photos was the most popular. I had to buy a few extra copies of them, also. That picture of Buddy with his chin in hand is absolutely one of the best ever of him and the time when it was taken renders it even more poignant. Also, as usual Bill Griggs had a large supply of goodies for sale.

Round about 6 PM, the display time was closed down, and about 9 PM came the 50's party – 50's dress optional. Entertainment was provided by a local rock trio called the Echoes of Holly –featuring Paul Waters on lead guitar and vocals (plus a bassist and drummer whose names I didn't catch). Average age of the group is 16. Paul Waters plays a Fender Stratocaster sunburst. He is tall and as skinny as Buddy was. For performances, Paul slicks his brown hair back in a semi-ducktail, curls falling over his forehead, and black glasses frames (without lenses). Resemblance is uncanny.

Though nervous at first, the band soon got cooking and really raved with the Holly rock and roll (ain't no better rock 'n' roll nowhere). After the band's first break, a film crew from the new TV show "World of People" came to film and interview us. They were not the only film crew to tape our activities, but they certainly were the most obnoxious. They seemed to have some stereotyped notion of how "Hollymaniacs" should behave and they were trying to make us conform to it by the questions that they asked and by trying to tell us what to say. The conceited, egoistical woman who did most of the talking was trying to run our party. They got some people to dance (Paul Waters and his band were nervous enough playing to their toughest critics, and the meddling media did not help). Once the dancers got on the floor (the band continued to play during all this); they went at it with gusto and really got down and boogied.

Well, her majesty [the woman from "World of People"] was trying to narrate an intro while walking through the dancers. She apparently expected them to part miraculously for her, like the Red Sea for Moses, so she could glide through. But she kept getting bumped by the dancers (usually by Penny Sue Falker and Nigel Smith, whose aim we admired). Every time she tried, she got bumped and then got mad. So one of the men in the film crew (the producer?) went up to the drummer of the Echoes of Holly and was giving the kid a hard time.

Finally the intruders left. The band got started up again and for the rest of the evening, they were dynamite. Their version of "Rave On" is fantastic!
Mary Ann videotaped most of their concert and afterwards, she invited the Echoes of Holly, Paul's parents, and a dozen or so other people up to our room to see the party on video tape. It was the first time that the boys had seen themselves on TV.
Next day was another display-buy-sell time, this time out on the patio as there were problems with the air-conditioning in the Gold Room. Larry Holley, Travis Holley, and their and Bud's sister Patricia showed up. Also Larry's daughter Sherry and Travis' daughter Travetta. In addition to selling LP's (lots of them), they signed autographs, answered questions, and posed for photographs. Travis' facial resemblance to Buddy is quite disturbing at times.

The statue unveiling was moved up from Saturday afternoon to Friday night just before the concert and just before sunset. So we went to the Lubbock Civic Center (a lovely, very new building) early and gathered around the covered statue. Mr. and Mrs. Holley, Larry, Travis, Patricia, Larry Corbin [of KLLL], and the sculptor, Grant Speed were there as were Maria Elena and other dignitaries. The unveiling ceremony was comparatively brief and plain but very nice (news cameras were out in force).
The statue does and does not look like Buddy. But it is an excellent work of art. As Grant Speed told us, Buddy had many different views when photographed from different angles.

The Green Bay Feb. 1, 59 photos were a great help to Mr. Speed. He also used Travis Holley as a model as Travis' facial bone structure is identical to Bud's.

Then we wandered around the Civic Center a little and bought programs. The Holley family had a table set up and were selling their LP. There were a few other tables selling sketches of Buddy, as well as Holly and [Roy] Orbison T-shirts.

Security personnel at the concert were a bit (!) confused. At one door – the North Door – for a while they were even confiscating still cameras, and protests about this by Bill Griggs and Don Larson were to no avail. But at the South Door, where I went in, there were no searches, and me and my little instamatic camera had no trouble getting in. Tape recorders were strictly forbidden, but I understand that several were smuggled in.
'The World of People" film crew was there. Someone had laid the law down to them and, though they continued filming us, they no longer tried to interfere. The concert itself was great! A whole evening jam-packed with good old rock and roll! First to come on was Bo Diddley. It's not for nothing that he is one of the fathers of rock and roll (as Charles H. Holley also was). He was really a-cookin'! That guy can rock! He is a past master of the electric guitar.

Next came on Roy Orbison. He started out a bit slow, but then really got going! When his voice was going full blast, I thought the amps would blow! He did the final part of "Running Scared" three times because the audience liked it so much. There is an electricity, an excitement, a rapport, in a good live concert that just cannot come across on recordings. That's why we like rock and roll; most exciting and best music around!

Next came the Crickets with very little announcement. It took us a moment to realize that their guest rhythm guitarist was Waylon Jennings unannounced and without star billing. This shows the depths of his feelings for Buddy, that he, a superstar, would make an unannounced appearance in honor of his friend.

The Crickets set was too short, otherwise it was the crowning achievement of the evening. Sonny really got raving on the guitar on "Slippin' and Slidin'" and "Keep-a-Knockin'" !
We jumped in our seats; clapped our hands; yelled; slapped our knees; stood up and danced, and generally made a helluva lot of noise and thoroughly enjoyed ourselves.
It needed only one person to have really completed the show. The person who was missing is Buddy Holly.

Next day, Sept. 6, at 10 AM was the memorial service at the grave. The BHMS bouquet – white flowers in the shape of a cross – was already in place, and someone had put a large picture of Buddy next to it. A DJ friend of Barb Rau's had recorded the taped part of the service for us, an excellent job. Mike Oestreicher of Flagstaff AZ conducted the live part of the service. The inevitable news cameras were there, even in our moment of deep, intense, private, personal grief. The "World of People" groups were a bit better behaved but had no concept of respect for the dead.

At the end of the ceremony, all who had flowers came forward and put them on the grave. There were so many flowers and bouquets that the gravestone was partially obscured by them.

Not long after we got back to the hotel, Larry Holley showed up with Bud's Stratocaster, and everyone had to see it and touch it. Gene Ammons handed Buddy's guitar to me (so my picture could be taken), and I was afraid I would drop it! Although I had held this guitar last year, the thrill of holding it again was just as great! Just to touch something that belonged to Buddy!

Also Mrs. Holley, Travis, Sherry [Larry's daughter], Travetta [Travis' daughter], and Maria Elena all came. We were all milling around on the patio, talking to them, taking pictures, getting autographs, and asking the inevitable questions. Paul Waters and his band were there, but as fans not as performers and dressed as 80's teenagers.

A singer, whose name escapes me, being sponsored by Larry Holley, was allowed to plug Bud's guitar into an amp, and he sang some -he is good. Then he played while Sherry Holley sang a few of her uncle's songs. We all agreed that she should record an LP of her Uncle Buddy's songs as she does them very well. Then Paul Waters got to play Buddy's guitar, as did Walter Reynolds, and Larry Holley. For a 58 Stratocaster, it plays very well. However, none of those who played it that afternoon could do it anywhere near as good as the original owner. Then came early evening, in time for the convention. We started out in the Gold Room but eventually had to move to the patio as the air-conditioning was still acting up. Kay Larson and Susan Short brought in two cakes, one in the shape of a Stratocaster was Bud's birthday cake. We also sang "Happy Birthday" to him, then. Susan Long won the T-shirt contest; Dave Pemberton won the poster contest, and Jack Miller (who couldn't get to Lubbock) won the poetry contest. Bill Griggs had a raffle drawing, 100 prizes. Several people won a number of prizes. But Suzie [me] won one, a set of back issues of the newsletter ["Reminiscing"].

Then we had another party in the Gold Room (the air-conditioning functioned somewhat) with Paul Waters and the Echoes of Holly. While they were taking their break, Joey Allen performed. Both do Holly music excellently.

A few of us hardy souls, on finding that the movie was showing at midnight went to the theater in a van and a car or two, maybe 15 - 20 of us. Just before the movie started at midnight, we sang "Happy Birthday" to Buddy. This particular print that this theater had wasn't in the best of shape, but I still enjoyed watching the movie for the 10th time, watching it in Lubbock on Buddy's birthday.

Bill Griggs gave his Holly slide show the next day, the 7th of Sept., Buddy Holly's 44th birthday. Good show.

There were about 100 Holly fans from 39 states and 8 countries – England, Wales, Ireland, Holland, Germany, Canada, France, and Australia.

Special thanks to Don Larson and his planning committee for doing such an excellent job of organizing everything. Special thanks to Bill Griggs for his efforts in helping the convention run smoothly.

Thanks also to the Holley family and Maria Elena for taking the time to meet with us and for having patience with our sometimes overwhelming Holly enthusiasm.
Thanks also to the performers for dy-no-mite concerts and performances.
But most of all, thank you, Buddy, for giving us that wonderful music, and we all love you and miss you more with each passing day. Thank you for just being Buddy Holly.

Sue Frederick

I first met Buddy Holly in fourth grade and then we hooked up in junior high. He and Bob Montgomery played and sang for our assemblies. The summer between Jr. Hi and Hi School we became a threesome. The guys would come by my house and we would play ping-pong and then go get a Coke at a drive-in. Whenever school started, I was allowed to start dating. Buddy and Bob would vie to see who would get Friday night for the football game and who would get Saturday night for a movie.

I quit dating Bob later that year, but continued to date Buddy regularly, although I also dated other guys from church. My mother discouraged the practice of going steady with just one guy because of the familiarity and pressure it puts on a couple. Buddy and I continued to date throughout high school and into my first two years at college.

My freshman year of college, I attended Abilene Christian University in Abilene Tx, just a three hour drive from Lubbock. So, Buddy and I were able to see other frequently during that year. I came home fairly often on week-ends and he also visited me on campus. The following year, however my roommate and I transferred to a small Christian Liberal Arts College in York, NE. The added distance from Lubbock meant that I would only be going home once during the semester, at Christmas. We were both busy, me with my studies and Buddy working towards recognition in the music industry. A highlight of that fall term was when he surprised me with a visit to the campus. That really helped to break up the long semester of being separated. I returned to Lubbock for the summer months and had looked forward to spending more time with Buddy. However most of his summer was spent doing more recordings in Clovis and on tours in the Northeast. He also did several shows in Carlsbad, NM where I now live. He had an aunt and uncle here that later I became friends with. The summer went quickly and then I was back at York College for my junior year. A carload of new guys from Montana descended upon the college campus for the second semester, although one of them was from Missouri. He had ended up in Montana while working the wheat harvest. When the fall term started, he stayed there to work in order to help his younger brother with tuition money so he could attend college. The Montana boys talked him into going with them to Nebraska. Since I was the receptionist for the school, I was the first girl he met on campus.

I guess the rest is history, as Ron and I got to know one another our love grew. We sat in the parlor of the girls' dorm and watched Buddy perform on the Ed Sullivan Show. I was excited about the recognition and popularity that he was gaining through his music, but I also recognized that it was creating a separation in the goals and aspirations that I had for my life. Breaking up with Buddy was very difficult, because we truly loved each other, but I also knew God had other plans for my life. News of Buddy's death was very difficult for me. Ron and I had been married just shy of one year. I was a senior at the University Of Montana and was student-teaching second grade that quarter. I was getting ready for school that morning when my mother called to give me the tragic news

Blessings - Echo McGuire Griffith

I first saw Buddy & the Crickets Sept. 13, 1957 at Hershey, PA "Sports Arena." They were with the Irvin Feld "Biggest Show of Stars", Fall, '57 edition. I spoke briefly with J.I. backstage about the difference between "The Crickets" and "Buddy Holly" recordings. J.I. explained that "The Crickets" backed up Buddy on "everything." He seemed kinda shy.

I saw them again May 9, 1958 in Hershey as part of an Alan Freed package tour. This was the tour that was involved in a "riot" in Boston a few nights earlier. I was backstage for most of this appearance and talked with everyone on the tour. Buddy was very soft-spoken. We talked about "Rave On" and "Take Your Time" and the fact that Norman Petty played organ on "Take Your Time." Buddy was only too happy to pose for pictures and sign autographs.

I was right next to him as he ripped off a couple of chords on his Fender Stratocaster right before going on stage. I also watched as J.I. and Joe B. participated in a lively game of "craps" in the dressing room. J.I. and Joe B. didn't say much. It didn't occur to me to ask why Niki Sullivan wasn't with them. As the performers left the building for the bus, Buddy and J.I. were the last two I said "Goodbye" to. Didn't realize the significance of that "goodbye" until 10 months later.

Bob Lee

On stage at the Sports Arena, Hershey, Pennsylvania - May 9, 1958

Backstage at the Sports Arena, Hershey, Pennsylvania - May 9, 1958

On stage at the Sports Arena, Hershey, Pennsylvania - May 9, 1958

On stage at the Sports Arena, Hershey, Pennsylvania - May 9, 1958

Backstage at the Sports Arena, Hershey, Pennsylvania - May 9, 1958

Backstage at the Sports Arena, Hershey, Pennsylvania - May 9, 1958

On stage at the Sports Arena, Hershey, Pennsylvania - May 9, 1958

I have been a fan of Buddy since a very young age. I grew up around early rock and roll. I dare not call it 50's music because it dates it and those songs last forever.
My earliest recollection of buying any Buddy Holly music was a year or two before La Bamba came out I bought the Buddy Holly collection on tapes. I believe there were 6 tapes in the collection and ever since then I was hooked. I take Buddy Holly very seriously and mostly get in quarrels over who is better Buddy or Elvis, and everyone knows who I would pick.

Buddy being born a Virgo and me being a Virgo I have a connection to him and it don't matter what mood, I'm in either if I'm sad or happy, Buddy has a song for me. I'm a singer in a band and although my music is quite different than Buddy's there is a little influence. I really wanted to attend this Winter Dance Party in Clear Lake but I guess I'll settle for the 75th Anniversary another 25 years later.

Those three were a true inspiration even if people started liking them because of the movies or because of the horrible crash that ended their live so sudden. It was so complete that now no one takes their music for granted. Buddy Holly lives on with every ear that will listen and to every song that is played and because people like us never truly let the music die!!!!

Matthew Fox 2009

My father was in the military. When I was in high school, he got stationed in Lubbock, TX. I had seen the Buddy Holly Story when I was a kid and heard him on the radio, so I was aware of Buddy's music. But when you live here it becomes a part of you. It enters your bloodstream.

Now I'm close friends with Buddy's niece Ingrid and his songs are very dear to us all.

Scott Faris   2009

I was really into "That'll Be The Day". Our local (very conservative) radio station wouldn't play rock 'n roll, so we had to listen to the only am radio station we could receive at nighttime that played r 'n r, and that was KOMA Oklahoma City. However, the local station would play Norman Petty Trio music - "Almost Paradise". Strange that I heard that recording quite a few times on the local station but never paid attention to the title of the song, or the name of the artist. When we got to Clovis for our first recording session at the Norman Petty studio, he played their recording of "Almost Paradise", and I about fell over in astonishment... "I know that song... that's you guys???... wow how neat - I really like that song" ! ! .....

My first interest (1946-47) came from hearing a group of harmonica players on the radio - the Harmonicats playing the song "Peg Of My Heart". About the same timeframe my Mom would pick out one finger tunes on the family piano. And she would experiment with two fingers, but I didn't know at the time that was called harmony. I just knew two fingers sounded better than one. My music came from my Mom's side of the family. She could sing with the radio, play two finger piano, and liked to dance. Next, what really caught my ear was the song "Guitar Boogie Shuffle" by either Guitar Boogie Smith, or the Virtues. I was too young to pay attention to whose recording it was. One day in (Columbian) grade school, we had a short assembly. It was two local musicians - the Amadeo brothers - playing "Guitar Boogie Shuffle" live with electric guitars through one amplifier ! Wow ! That's the song that sent me goofy on playing guitar ! ! And then hearing Les Paul (& Mary Ford) just fueled my desire and interest for more guitar. Chet Atkins was one of my favorites to listen to also, but I never did pursue his finger picking style of playing. Just really loved listening to it. Then in 1958 in college in Socorro, New Mexico at the Institute of Mining & Technology, I wrote my first guitar song, "Fireball", which I heard in a dream. I woke up enough to get my electric 'unplugged' guitar out of the case and try to figure out how to play the melody I just dreamed about, which I finally did. And that turned out to be one side of our first 45 rpm vinyl recording, released in Jan '59 on Kapp Records.

Ritchie had a very distinctive guitar sound at the beginning of that record... unbelievable! I remember thinking that he was the first r 'n r Hispanic guy (that I knew of) to hit the big time - and I really liked him.

When Chantilly Lace came on the radio I was impressed that it was a really different lyric song - with an unusual melody and a little bit of 'talk singing' in it. That used to fascinate me... how could anyone think of all those different kinds of things to write in a song, and then perform it so well ! !

George Tomsco (The Fireballs -2009)

I discovered the music quite by accident. Though I had records I collected from when I first remember, especially in 1956, I completely missed out on 1957 as I was just totally involved with swimming as an activity. I had been listening to the radio on a regular basis for only a couple of months when I first heard the name Buddy Holly. I went into my local record shop, saying I wanted "Early In The Morning" by Bobby Darin and the Rinky Dinks (giving her the full name pretty, impressive for a 9 year old). The owner of the store called Walden's music, Annetta Berman, said "I like Buddy Holly's version 'cause I can understand the words better." She played it, pulling out that Coral label and I wondered "Who's Buddy Holly?", but kept it to myself. Then I didn't know which one to buy and bought neither. It was only years later that I realized I had heard "Rave On" being played loudly emerging from a pool hall/bar in Long Beach. I'll get to Long Beach later. I found a copy of "Peggy Sue" in Walden's, played it and "Everyday" over the sound system and knew I had to have it. A little later I saw a picture of Buddy Holly in the back of the store. Then right around this time, right as I started school, I was listening in the morning before I was to walk the mile to elementary school, when I heard a deejay announce a flashback, "That'll Be The Day" by the Crickets from one year ago. It just totally knocked me out !! The following Sunday, while visiting my great Aunt Sue, I found "The Chirping Crickets" EP ,featuring it along with "I'm Looking For Someone To Love", "Oh Boy", and "Not Fade Away" , at the Thrifty Drug Store record dept where some rack jobber had placed it. It wasn't until I got it home and flipped it over, reading the liner notes, that I found out this same Buddy Holly was the leader of the Crickets.

Around Christmas time, I saw a copy of "Heartbeat" in the May Co.'s basement record dept next to "The Chipmunk Song" (ironic that I was to find out years later what a big fan Buddy Holly was of the Chipmunks). Buddy Holly was probably my favorite artist at the time. I enjoyed what he did under the moniker of the Crickets as my very favorites, but they all rank high up there. My standards for Buddy are very high indeed.

I first heard Ritchie Valens with "Come On Let's Go" on KPOP, 'Your official El Monte Legion stadium station", as they called themselves. Then next on KFWB, which was the first ever radio station to play it, on "The Ted Quillan Show". Yes, I was a fan immediately, and knew Ritchie Valens was Chicano, or Mexican-American from the getgo, having lived originally in East L.A. in my earliest years. When I heard "La Bamba", I didn't know he didn't speak Spanish. "Donna" rose to #1 in L.A. in December of 1958. After I heard about the plane crash, I went out and purchased at the May Co. the LP "Ritchie Valens". This conflicts with the official record which states it was released in mid-March. I knew I couldn't have bought the LP then as I was in the burn ward of Childrens' Hospital, being treated for third degree burns starting March 6. In my convalescence at home, KFWB would play "That's My Little Suzie", always referring to him as "the late, great Ritchie Valens".

I first saw the Big Bopper's name on the jukebox at Margarita's Mexican Restaurant, where my parents and I would always dine. I was intrigued by "Purple People Eater Meets The Witch Doctor" as I was eight going on nine and a lover of novelty records, like most kids my age. Then they flipped it over and started playing "Chantilly Lace", which I would always hear and dug on the weekends on the car radio, going down to Long Beach with my parents to visit Aunt Sue. When "Big Bopper's Wedding" came out, I was digging it on KDAY and my mother came in and said "Turn down that racket; that's awful."

It really is ironic that she became later such a fan of the Big Bopper when I took her to see "The Buddy Holly Story". She even clipped out a magazine ad with a reference to Chantilly!

My thoughts as the anniversary approaches is that I would love to be up at Clear Lake to commemorate it. Ironically Dodie Stevens is on the show and I saw her singing at a Cub Scout Convention at the Shrine Auditorium (where the Crickets performed in 1957) only a few weeks before I was burned.

Mark Deaver (2009)

I discovered Buddy Holly when I was 10 years old back in 1970

Until then I thought that I had heard what you call good music but I was wrong. Listening to my brother's album for the first time was like an awakening. I can remember like it was yesterday listening to That'll Be The Day and thinking this is real music. I was taken over by it so that each and every day, I would come home from school to get my fix and put the record on. All I used to think about at school was being in a band like Buddy's. I would compare all other music by the standard that Buddy Holly set.

I have been known as a Buddy Holly tribute artist for many years. But even now his music means the world to me. The magic has never worn off. Its not easy to explain because the combination of Buddy's vocals, his taste in music, and the quality of the musicianship and recording technique all come together to make something timeless.

Graham Holly

J P was a very talented songwriter and a model deejay. His stage and radio persona of The Big Bopper never really gave people an idea of who he really was or what he was really like, which was quite the opposite of the Bopper.

Their musical influence is heard in almost any kind of music you hear today, whether the artists creating the music realize it or not. These were three pioneers who paved the way for entire styles and generations of music.

Jim McCool

This was one of the mysteries of that night. My wife took a dozen or so pictures ALL turned out blank!!! The camera, while ancient today, still functions perfectly, except for that night.

Just as Buddy got into Carroll Anderson's car for the ride to the airport he said "I will be in touch about a Summer Dance Party as soon as I get home, see you then, and have lots of brats for us". Sam Geller the road manager also said he hoped he could be on the trip, as he was delighted too with Bratwurst, a first for all those folks.

Bob Hale

March 21, 1958

TELEVISION PROGRAMMES
THURSDAY EVENING — MARCH 27

6.0 NEWS HEADLINES
SPORTS NEWS
THE WEATHER

ON TRANSMITTERS SERVING THE AREAS:
6.10 News for Scotland, Northern Ireland and the English Regions

News from Wales: 6.15-6.20

6.20 STAR CHOICE
presents
GREER GARSON
in
'THE EAR-RING'

An attempt to settle with a blackmailer and the unfortunate loss of an ear-ring lead to serious complications.

A series of film plays presenting stars in stories of their choice.

—————ROWRIDGE—————
6.20 'IT'S MY OPINION'
A West-Country discussion programme with
John Connell, Percy Cudlipp
Anne Scott-James
Chairman, Jeremy Thorpe

—————ALL TRANSMITTERS—————
6.45 TONIGHT
Look around with
Cliff Michelmore
Sport—Music—People
Cinema—Theatre—Argument
with
Derek Hart
Geoffrey Johnson Smith
Macdonald Hastings
and this week,
Maxine Daniels
Noel Harrison
Produced by DONALD BAVERSTOCK

7.25 NEWS SUMMARY

7.30 JACK PAYNE
introduces
stars and personalities who are

OFF THE RECORD
together with the latest news from the record industry
including
Buddy Holly
and the Crickets
Ronnie Hilton
Spike Milligan
The Mudlarks
Brendan O'Dowda
Diane Todd
and
George Melly
with Mick Mulligan's Band
with the Concert Orchestra and the George Mitchell Singers
Conducted by Stanley Black
Produced by JAMES GILBERT
(Buddy Holly and the Crickets were specially telerecorded for this programme)

Joyce Heron as Barbara Lomax, and John Arnatt as Bill Ogden

'Background'
A PLAY BY
Warren Chetham-Strode
adapted for television by the author
PRODUCED BY CAMPBELL LOGAN

Nanny Braun .... LILLY KANN
Linda Lomax .... INGRID SYLVESTER
Adrian Lomax .... CAVAN KENDALL
Jess Lomax .... MAVIS SAGE
Barbara Lomax .... JOYCE HERON
Bill Ogden .... JOHN ARNATT
John Lomax .... MICHAEL GWYNN
Police Constable ...... SIDNEY MONCKTON

Designer, Lawrence Broadhouse

The action takes place in the Lomax's house near London. TIME: The present

AT 8.30

8.0 GET AHEAD
The *News Chronicle* offers
£7,500
to
'Go Getters'

Televised each week direct from the public hearing in London as contestants answer the question
'How would you spend £5,000 to get ahead?'
Tonight the second finalist will be found by

Judges:
Sir Frederic Hooper
The Viscountess Lewisham
(Mrs. Gerald Legge)
The Earl of Halsbury

Chairman,
Peter West
hands £100 to the winner to be spent in seven days

Presented for television and directed by
DEREK BURRELL-DAVIS
From the Carlton Rooms, Maida Vale

8.30 MICHAEL GWYNN
JOYCE HERON
JOHN ARNATT
LILLY KANN
in
'BACKGROUND'
See top of page and page 4

L. C. Baker
LONDON

R. J. Rice
DIDCOT

N. D. Svendsen
BRIDGWATER

Three of the contestants in GET AHEAD at 8.0

10.0 NEWS
and
BEHIND THE HEADLINES

10.20 PIA SEBASTIANI
gives a piano recital of music by
Albeniz, Fauré
Debussy, Villa-Lobos
and Ginastera

10.35 THE BEST OF BENNY
starring
JACK BENNY
in the film series of top-line comedy shows
This week:
'Invited to the Colmans'
Mr. and Mrs. Ronald Colman are the guest stars and Jack tries ever so hard to be their guest.

11.0 NEWS SUMMARY
Including a film report from the Netherlands of today's events in
The State Visit
(Presented in co-operation with Nederlandse Televisie Stichting)

11.15 app. Weather
Road Works Report
and Close Down

On March 27th 1958 I was sitting in our living room with my parents. I was already quite a Crickets fan but had not realised that Buddy Holly was part of that group. We watched the news and then at 7.30pm the Jack Payne Show came on, a general variety show that usually had a bit of pop content, or even rock'n'roll content. Payne introduced Buddy Holly and The Crickets. I sat up; I had not known they were going to appear as I had not looked in the Radio Times. As we only had one channel on our TV at that time it was lucky we were watching but it would have been either that or the radio... or playing cards.

I found out later that the Crickets appearance had been filmed a couple of weeks earlier but that didn't matter anyway ... there they were. They performed "Maybe Baby" and I suppose you could say at that point I was hooked on Buddy & The Crickets for life. At least that's how it turned out. I don't remember Buddy or anyone else saying anything.
Actually, to be honest I don't remember much about the performance. There seemed to be a lot of sparkling lights and the set was quite flashy. And Buddy seemed incredibly tall and the whole thing was, well, cool. But other than that the only thing I remember is going out to buy "Maybe Baby" as soon as I could the next day, I think after school, on a 78rpm record purchased from the general music store in Dorking, Surrey, our nearest town. They were quite often out of stock of current records that had been featured on TV, and I remember feeling pleased that I managed to get a copy. By then 78s were fading; I was offered a 45, but we didn't have a suitable gramophone to play those. When I got home and heard the other side, "Tell Me How", wow, I knew I had made a good choice. I played both sides, over and over and over.

I don't remember anything else about the show, although I would have been interested in seeing comedian Spike Milligan, one of the radio 'Goons'. I have been a lifetime fan of his too but again, I was aware of him before the programme. The appearance of The Crickets that evening was really something special to me ... I just wish I could remember a bit more detail. And of course a video recorder would have come in handy if they had been invented at that time...

John Beecher

OFF THE RECORD
together with the latest news from the record industry
including
Buddy Holly and the Crickets

During the summer of 1971 I spent a couple of weeks at my Aunt's house. It was during this vacation that I discovered she had several old records from groups this kid had never heard of before. Among her many LPs she had 'The Everly Brothers', 'The Buddy Holly Story' and several other albums and a couple of 45's from the 1950s and 1960s.

I asked her if it was ok for me to listen to her records and she said it was. Little did this eleven year old boy realize that within seconds I was about to embark on a musical journey that would continue for the rest of my life.

Which album should I play first? I decided to listen to the 'Buddy Holly Story'. I was intrigued by the close-up of Buddy with his trademark glasses and movie star good looks. Once the needle touched the record, and Buddy began to sing, I fell in love with the music and played the album over and over again. So many times in fact, I was worried about breaking the needle. It was during that vacation that I knew the music would be with me for the rest of my life.

The year is 2007 and I began to think back to that summer vacation at my Aunt's house, almost forty years ago. It not only brought back a lot of good memories, it also brought a smile to my face when I thought back to how I discovered Buddy's music.

I will tell you without hesitation that I still feel like that eleven year old boy who fell in love with Buddy's music that summer vacation.

And just like that eleven year old boy, I still can't get enough of Buddy's music.

Gary Clevenger 2007

FOREVER 22

Verse 1:
Well, he really could sing and his voice would ring
When he sang to the beat of a drum,
Played a wild guitar and was a great big star
When twenty-two years had come.
Well, the good ole boys and good ole girls
Had already gathered around,
And the cricket did sing like a bird on the wing
Before the beetles ever made a sound.

Chorus:
Forever twenty-two,
With songs about love not fading away
And love that's always true.
He's forever twenty-two,
He's twenty-two, going on forever.

Verse 2:
On a cold black night like a bird in flight
He fell with the falling snow.
Did the story end, or did it just begin
When he fell to the earth below?
Then twenty-two years of joy and tears
Stopped, but the music goes on,
And there's never been a day though the years fade away
When Buddy doesn't sing a song.

Chorus:
Forever twenty-two,
With songs about love not fading away
And love that's always true.
He's forever twenty-two,
He's twenty-two, going on forever.

Verse 3:
As the years go by in the blink of an eye,
He will always be the same.
Still tall and thin, with the black horn rims,
Singing "That's When You're Learning The Game"
He'll play the guitar and still be a star
As long as they shine in the sky.
He'll be twenty-two, and for me and for you,
His music will never die.

Chorus:
Forever twenty-two,
With songs about love not fading away
And love that's always true.
He's forever twenty-two,
He's twenty-two, going on forever.

Music and Lyrics by John W. Pickering
© 2000 John Pickering Music Co.

A Gentle Spirit in the Wind.

Sailing down the river of memories

where stars appear and shadows fall.

I met a friend a gentle spirit in the wind.

Some say your gone forever that'll be the day

cause memories live forever and love won't fade away.

Still the sun is out the sky is blue.

You're blue without Peggy, we're blue without you

when crickets chirp and angels sing we'll meet again.

A gentle spirit in the wind.

Gary L Clevenger

The first time that I heard of the death of Buddy was when I listened to the song "Tribute to Buddy Holly" by Mike Berry in 1961. Even the next LP "Reminiscing -Buddy Holly" (CORAL 97025 /July 1963) had no such information on the cover. We had to wait until Oct. 1963 when CORAL published the album "Buddy Holly -My Greatest Songs" (Coral 97028) and mentioned on the cover that he was killed in a plane crash on the 3rd February 1959. No word about where and why it happened or about Ritchie and The Big Bopper, who died with him, and the pilot Roger Peterson.

A booklet (Buddy Holly –We'll Always Remember/ Dutch and English text) by John C. Beecher and Jan Schijff from the mid 60s told us in the Dutch text that the plane crashed near Mason City ("Op 3 februari 1959 kwam hij om het leven, toen zijn vliegtuig neerstorrte in de omgeving van Mason City."). And again nothing about the fact that he didn't die alone. Zijn = his plane crashed - that's all we learned!! The English text only said: "3rd February 1959 he died in a plane crash ..." For the first time however we got to know, via this booklet, that he was born on 7th September 1936.

The cover of the LP "Buddy Holly" (CORAL 97030 / prob. 1964) told us that Norman Petty had a recording studio in Clovis, where "That'll Be The Day" had been recorded. And the home town of Buddy was Lubbock in Texas, as we could read.

From the cover of the Italian LP "Buddy Holly – 'It doesn't matter anymore' (SIR VAL 7008) we learned that Norman Petty was his manager and producer.

I discovered Rock 'n' Roll when I was only 10 years old. We had just escaped from the DDR (GDR) to the Western part of our country and I was struck by this type of music, the music of Elvis, Buddy Holly, Ritchie Valens, Eddie Cochran, Gene Vincent, Fats Domino, Little Richard, Jerry Lee Lewis, Bobby Vee etc. etc.

I had and still have the single of "La Bamba". One can't say they are a fan of somebody when there's only one record of this singer in his collection. But after having heard the complete story of the 3rd February 1959, I also began to collect the records of Ritchie as I had become a big fan of him too.

But let me say that from my point of view it was Rock 'n' Roll which changed the life of a whole generation and the generations to come. It was the beginning of a sort of a revolution against the so called war generations of our fathers and grandfathers. There were discussions like never before in the families, schools and churches I guess. The Rock 'n' Roll invented the wheel of music for a second time you even can say.

Lothar Pedd

My interest in Buddy Holly and my love of his music as well as 50s Rock 'n' Roll and the era in general has been with me for the last 30 something years almost my whole life.
It all can be traced back to 1957 when my 9 year old father heard "That'll Be The Day" and bought the 78 rpm record. My father from that point was a Buddy Holly and The Crickets fan and for the rest of the 50s and throughout the 60s and decades to follow would buy Buddy's albums and 45s and play them.

I am told by my mother that when she was pregnant with me, I would kick and move around whenever my dad would play Buddy's music along with other greats such as Eddie Cochran. This continued when I was very young listening to the music that came out of the speakers that towered above me.

Then in 1980 when I was 8 years of age my father bought our first video recorder and hired the "The Buddy Holly Story", which I sat and watched one afternoon. I remember watching the film loving the images in front of me and the reconstruction of the era and crying at the end when it seemed all over and asking my parents what happened to Buddy and realising that he had in fact died.
This moved me as he seemed very much alive to me. Being so young I had not realised until that moment that the music and the person I had heard and seen on many album covers had actually lived decades before as time had no meaning to me then. Nor did I know about the life story and musical journey that led to the music I liked so much being created.

It was a few months after this that one day at middle school I was asked by my teacher if I would be interested in learning an instrument. The choices were the usual violin or cello or guitar. The guitar was the obvious identifiable choice for me that felt right. My parents agreed to let me learn and bought me my first guitar.

From that moment on I lived and breathed the guitar learning very quickly, and it came so naturally. Finally, within a few months I was able to play along with the music I liked so much. Working through a "Buddy Holly Lives" music book that was bought for me, I would spend every spare moment playing Buddy's songs, striving to get every detail of playing right and wanting to re-produce the amazing sound that spoke so loudly to me.

Through my teenage years from 1986 I started to look into Buddy's life by reading every book that was available at that time, including the fabulous "Remembering Buddy" book which still stands as the best today. I was enthralled by the story and it took me on a journey and made my own journey of learning Buddy's music and music of the 50s so real to me, as if I was following the same footsteps.

At this time in the 1980s I should have been more immersed in the pop culture of the time. However, I could never identify with it and felt at home in the 50s, which I never knew first hand. I am sure this caused concern with people around me, like friends, but I could not help it.

I remember going to a local musical instrument store when I was about 14 and picking up a Hohner catalogue where they had a picture of a ST57 Strat guitar which was based on the 1957 sunburst Strat that I had seen on the cover of the "Chirping Crickets"album. I had to have it. Drooling over this catalogue for months and doing whatever jobs I could to save for the guitar, I finally managed to buy it. From this point I would sit in my bedroom at every waking moment and just try to learn all the lead breaks and down strokes that Buddy was showing me through his music. The joy I would feel when I nailed a particular song, feeling that I had achieved something !

In 1994 I had the opportunity in my job to win a place to fly to Dallas, Texas, for a week of training and fun. I saw this as an amazing chance to finally be near Lubbock and I worked hard and won my place. I arranged to stay out for another week and would spend that week in Lubbock. The wonderful thing was that my father decided that, through my interest in Buddy re-vitalising his own interest, he would join me in Lubbock. So began a father and son pilgrimage to find the real Buddy and to walk the streets and drive the roads that Buddy had, including houses, places of interest and Clovis.
Later in 2006, we went back to Lubbock again for Buddy's 70th Birthday and did the whole thing again, this time armed with a Sat Nav. On this trip we were staying at the Holiday Inn, that many who have been to Lubbock would know, and were amazed to find ourselves standing outside chatting with Tommy Allsup and his band. Tommy later invited me and my father to see them do an impromptu jam session in the hotel bar where I got to play a couple of songs on Tommy's acoustic guitar to the audience, which was a thrill.

Now bringing it forward to the present day, in 2008 I decided that I wanted to be a part of the 50th Anniversary of the Winter Dance Party in Clear Lake. I had for years been a regular member of Bill Griggs' board and saw many people sharing their stories of attending previous year's events and getting to talk to some of these people. Becoming friends online with them urged me to want to be a part of the biggest event - the 50th. Wearing many layers of clothing, we had an amazing time discovering the area, the Surf, the crash site and the airport where Buddy took off from. It was 1994 all over again, following in Buddy's footsteps, although it was sad to think that the footsteps we were following were his final steps.

Dan Springall

MEMORIES OF THE HI-D-HO DRIVE-IN RESTAURANTS

I grew up just 3 blocks (306 Avenue W) from the Hi-D-Ho #1 and spent some time over there. Since we lived so close, my parents would take us kids over there for burgers and treats. I can still see it so clearly in my mind. There was another Hi-D-Ho just a few blocks down from #1 that was lovingly called Hi-D-Ho Jr. (Unknown trivia: "That'll Be The Day" was actually conceived at the Jnr where there was inside dining.) Buddy and friends first started writing the song in a booth after watching the John Wayne movie, "The Searchers" at the Lindsey Theater which was downtown.

I was one of the Lubbockites that was fortunate enough to get to actually see Buddy and his friends playing on top of the Hi-D-Ho #1. They didn't play there long, only a couple of weeks, but it was "instrumental" in helping launch what was to eventually become one of the most beloved singers in music history. The Hi-D-Ho's were "round" buildings with cars parking all the way around. The teenagers would spend hours every day "cruising" round and round and round them, it was SO cool!!! Buddy and the boys were right in the middle of the cruising (actually performing on the front part of the building). And he spent much time cruising around the Hi-D-Ho's looking for a pretty girl to cruise with him. No telling how many miles they drove going around those places, yet never went anywhere! Needless to say, at the time I saw Buddy there, I had no earthly idea I was watching a star and a person who would be loved by so many all over the world.

Lubbock was not a very large "town" in those days, maybe 40,000 people, but it was far from the concept many people have of it being a little country town. We had 15 and 20 story buildings downtown even back then, so one can see that it wasn't a little country town. It now has over 200,000 population.

The Hi-D-Ho's are long gone. On the site where #1 once stood, (the street was College Avenue and 2nd St when Buddy was there, it is now University and 2nd) a Burger King now operates there. A new freeway is currently being built just a few feet from the parking lot of the Burger King.

Hi-D-Ho Jr. was across the railroad track, on the same side of the street just north of the famous skating rink where Buddy used to sing. They are actually only a few feet apart. A "Tommy's Burger" parking lot is now where Hi-D-Ho Jnr was located. The Hi-D-Ho (original), Jr. and the skating rink were all on the same side of the street (east side of College Avenue), and all were in close proximity to each other.

As for the "new" Hi-D-Ho, it was built sometime in the 1990's and was in a new part of Lubbock, far away from where the originals were. When it was built, they made the mistake of not making it round, it simply looked like every other rectangle restaurant building, with a few angles in the front, but it just didn't look like the real one's and didn't have a lot of space immediately around the building to park. It didn't last very long. I think if it had been built as a replica of the #1, it probably would still be in operation today. It did have a large amount of Buddy memorabilia in it, but that was the only thing that even remotely made it a Hi-D-Ho. It is now an auto dealership. The Hi-D-Ho's are truly a piece of Lubbock and Buddy Holly history.

GRAND OPENING OF THE TOWN AND COUNTRY SHOPPING CENTER

Across the street directly west of where the original Hi-D-Ho stood on College Avenue, the first large "strip" shopping center in Lubbock was built in the mid 1950's. The name of the shopping center was Town and Country. I remember what a big deal it was when they were building it and how happy we were that we would have a real nice, big grocery store by the name of Furr Food to open up so close to our house, still at 306 Avenue W. There was a bakery in the shopping center which was known as Snowhite Bakery (I can still see the neon lit fairytale figure of Snowhite). I'll never forget how good their cakes were! Of course there were many other nice stores in the center as well.

One of the highlights of my life was during the grand opening of Town and Country Center. I will never forget my mother and daddy taking me and my brother over there to the grand opening celebration. It was a BIG deal! Once again, I was watching Buddy Holley perform, and again, had no idea I was watching a star in the making. Buddy and the "Original Crickets" were performing on a cotton trailer which had the sideboards removed so that it was just a flat stage. Several bales of alfalfa hay was stacked next to the trailer to make a stairway so the musicians could get on and off of the trailer. I thought those hay bales had been put there for my personal use, so I was playing around on them, going up and down, laughing and having a great time, not thinking about anything except what a good time I was having. I would stop for a minute or two to watch the performers, and then get back to my playing. I'll never forget one time when I climbed too high and got near the top, and Buddy yelled at me, "Little girl, you need to stay off the hay and away from the trailer so you won't get hurt!" Being the obedient child that I was, I got down and never went near the trailer again. Of course I was embarrassed and finished out the evening hiding behind my parents. But that is a vivid memory that will be cherished forever.

BUDDY AND THE BOWLING ALLEYS

My daddy operated a couple of bowling alleys in downtown Lubbock, one being the Lubbock Bowling Club and the other was Playmore Lanes. My mom was a working mom, even back in the 1950's, at American State Bank. Daddy would take me and my brother with him to the bowling alleys to keep us entertained. These were back in the days before automatic pen setters and the bowling pens were known as "duckpens". They were a bit more squatty than current-day pens and had a rubber ring around the large part of the pen. Daddy had a couple sets of these kind of pens special made for me and my brother (scaled down in size for children) and he had little ebonite balls (scaled for us) also made and finger holes drilled in them especially for us kids. He would set us up over on the far side away from the regular customers so we could bowl and he had a special person behind the pens to reset them when we would be fortunate enough to hit some.

Buddy and his friends would frequent the bowling alleys. They would bowl several games, play the pinball machines and just hang around and kill time, doing whatever it was that boys did back in those days. He was a teenager at the time. My friend, Tinker Carlen, recalled watching me and my brother over on our side of the building. It wasn't unusual for them to come over and watch us and play with us. They thought it was so cute to see the little kids having their own little bowling setup and having fun and would talk about those cute little kids bowling. And again, I had a brush with one of the most beloved and best known musicians of all time, and naturally had no idea I was in the presence of greatness.

These are a fond memories I have of seeing and being in the presence of Buddy Holly.

Glenda Ward

Four days after my fifteenth birthday……

Alarm clock ringing, ringing, ringing
Stretch, yawn, stretch
Rub the sleep from my eyes
Mother calls
Breakfast on the table in 10 minutes
Must move, kick the blankets off
It is cold in here
Full of February cold
No heating
Heat downstairs – kitchen, living room
And in the bowl of porridge on the table
Another day at school
Rush to the bathroom and run the water
Oh dear, it's Wednesday
Oh dear, double maths, late morning
Rush to the bedroom
Pull on cold clothes
Glad the homework is done
Satchel ready to go
Mum calls – urgently
The bowl of porridge is on the table
It will be too hot to eat now!
Hurry downstairs anyway
Hope Avril is back at school
Missed her yesterday
Into the warm, welcoming kitchen
Bowl of porridge steams on the table
Glance at the 'paper on the side
Daily Mirror
Photo' of a man with outstretched arms
Another smaller photo'
"Top 'Rock' Stars Die In Crash"
Mother says sit and eat
Too hot just yet, Mum
Reach for the 'paper and read
Stunned……
Killed
Buddy Holly
Big Bopper
Ritchie Valens
Read – don't believe
Drop the paper and sit at the table
Can't be true – must be true – can't be….
Mum says eat, it is getting cold
Pick up the spoon and scoop up hot porridge
Why did they take off in a snowstorm?
Sugar, no sugar?

No…..thanks, Mum.
Why? ……. in a snowstorm
The bowl is empty - drop the spoon
Feel sick
You'll miss the bus if you don't leave now
Yes, Mum – bye

Get to school – the bell rings
Head down and into assembly
Everything as normal, but it isn't – is it?
Headmaster goes on – about……
Why? Why did they fly, in a snowstorm?
Registration
Yes, here, but not – feel…… one step away

History first? Then RI or maybe geography?
Where is the timetable?
C'mon Gib' – RI with Jock, then history with Webby
No more records, no more songs, no more……
Maybe it's a mistake, someone's silly……
No, it's not April 1 today.

Keep quiet, head down
Jock is jabbering, telling all about……
Everything drifts past – past
Mason City - Fargo, North Dakota
Where are they?
Must be colder than here - snow everywhere?
Why play out there, in the cold?
Then it's Webby and…… something about….
Mid-morning break
Hey Gib', playing football?
No, no thanks
Wander off to a quiet corner
A few there already
Heads down, hands in pockets
No one talking
Stewart is there
He looks up and nods
Seen the news in the 'paper?
Can't say anything – just nod
He turns and wanders away
What to say?

The lessons roll on
Next, maths with Relton - algebra
Last Monday with Relton – a bad day, a strange day
Expecting worse from him today
Nothing – he looks elsewhere
Sit quietly and the lesson flows by
Does Relton know……something?
The bell rings – lesson over

Lunch break
Eat the food then escape to the playground
More football – no, not playing
Same corner, same group
Same long faces, same silence
Same cold, same sadness
Same thought - why?

If they had gone by coach……
If the pilot had…… had……
If they'd waited until……
If…. If…. If….

The afternoon is here – English, French, then……
The mind wanders
Memories of the Palladium show
He seemed a bit nervous
Sang well though
Great songs
Great guitar
Great!
And that photo', Dad's great photo'
But now – no more shows
No more new songs - ever

Get home at last
Oh, was Avril at school?
Didn't see her – forgot to look
'Paper is in the sitting room
Read again, and again
Still the same story
Must be true, must be
But on Friday
Maybe the NME will tell more
Explain, maybe
Need to play some records
A stack of 45s

To lose a friend you've never met – so painful
A friend who speaks just to you
A friend who touches your spirit
A friend who helps
A friend who understands
A friend who is there anytime, every time
A friend you can rely on
A friend, who is now gone.

Wednesday, 4th February, 1959.
Just another day - for millions, just another day
But, for some, a day never to be forgotten
A day that changes everything - for ever.

Peter Gibson, Harrow, UK

"Of all the unique oddities of my career, I am perhaps proudest of the fact that I am forever linked with Buddy Holly. ... Buddy was a huge part of my childhood dream. Long before I decided how I would use music or what kind of artist I would be, Buddy was there. When I listened to his music, a mood overtook me which was both happy and sad, and I often looked at the record covers while the music played. "Buddy's music is so musical. The number of great recordings he made in his very short life places him at or beyond the level of any musical artist in almost any category. Elvis never wrote songs, while Buddy composed a large number. In my opinion, looking back, no rock act, not the Beatles, not the Stones, nor anyone else, can top records like 'Peggy Sue' or 'Rave On.' They are Rock Mountains that nobody has climbed.

The diversity of Buddy's music is also profound. 'Moondreams' and 'True Love Ways' are musically as advanced as anything by the great popular composers. Gershwin or Berlin would have marveled at these compositions.

Don Mclean

Lennon was contacted by Los Angeles music journalist Jim Dawson in 1974. Dawson asked a few questions pertaining to Buddy Holly:

How did you personally react to the Crickets' tour of England in 1958?
JL: "I only saw them on the London Palladium (on TV). He was great! It was the first time I saw a Fender guitar being played! While the singer sang! Also the 'secret' of the drumming on 'Peggy Sue' was revealed live."

What effect do you think it had on British musicians?
JL: "I only know its effect on me, but I reckon the records had the biggest effect on all of us. Every group tried to be The Crickets! The name Beatles was directly inspired by Crickets (double entendre/insects etc.). I think the greatest effect was on the songwriting."

What do you think of Buddy Holly, musically and historically?
JL: "He was a great and innovative musician. He was a MASTER! His influence continues. I often wonder what his music would be like now, had he lived."

Do you think his music had any effect on the style of The Beatles? On your own feelings toward music?
JL: "See above. We did practically everything he put out, i.e. at The Cavern, etc. What he did with three chords made a songwriter out of me!"

John Lennon

I would go to bed with Ritchie's record next to me, and cry myself to sleep; I would wake up the same way

Connie Lemos

When Ritchie was about fourteen, it amazed me how good he was, he could really play his guitar

Bob Morales

Ritchie was meticulous about his appearance, his guitar and shoes were always gleaming. He was always polishing his guitar and his shoes

Connie Lemos

Ritchie, always smelled like Old Spice, and he had very soft lips

Donna Ludwig Fox

I was working at KSST in Sulphur Springs when Buddy died, and it was painful because the Bopper had just performed in Sulphur Springs shortly before the crash and I had had a long talk with him backstage. He talked about missing his wife and his unborn child. He wanted to be at home in Beaumont with his family. He did tell me that he was heading out to the Winter Dance Party tour for the money, to provide a better life for his young family.

Paul Beane

Longtime radio personality in Lubbock. Byers has worked at KLLL-AM, KDAV-AM, KSEL-AM, KFYO-AM, KCAS-AM, KCBD-AM, KKCL-FM KZZN-FM

I first saw Buddy Holly in 1954 when my parents took me to the KDAV (580 AM) studio to watch Buddy, Bob and Larry perform on the Sunday party. He sang only country music on the radio.

Larry Byers

Lubbock native and Texas music producer and steel guitarist
I don't remember when I first heard Buddy's music on the radio. But the first time that I really paid attention to his music was when I started playing with Joe Ely. Joe did some Buddy Holly songs and I really started appreciating Buddy's writing.
It seemed that Buddy's music has no boundaries, and he obviously did not let it bother him when people dissed him for doing that "sinful" rock 'n' roll music. He stayed with what was in his heart and soul. Buddy paved the way for other artists and writers to create their art and not be afraid

Lloyd Maines

Your brother never forgot who he was, or where he came from, he was a very humble young man.

Dick Clark (American Bandstand) to Connie Lemos (Ritchie's Sister)

Mama worked to support us. Ritchie was our mother father and our brother. He was only seventeen, and he looked after us.

Connie Lemos

My fondest memories of Ritchie, was when he would take my sister and I outside and taught us The Paddiwack Song.

Irma Norton

About five or six Ritchie began to take an interest in music, he would carry around this little guitar, he started playing and kept playing, and he started sounding very good after a while.

Bob Morales

There was always music in our house, mama loved Rock and Roll and country, we even played Hawaiian music in our house, and can you believe that

Irma Norton

Ritchie would never sing his songs the same way twice. He was always trying new things with his music

Bob Morales

At Norman Petty's studio, it was on Wednesday, Sept. 3, 1958. After setting up the amplifiers and microphones about 4 p.m., we went down to Foxy's to grab a burger, and then come back to start recording. When we got back to the studio, there was a pink Cadillac with Texas plates parked in front of the studio, and we wondered who was there.

When we walked in, there was a strange looking guy with dark rimmed glasses playing my brand new Fender Strat with his foot up on my brand new Fender Tremolux Amp. I was ticked off to say the least.

He was playing my new guitar better than I could. Humiliating! I addressed Norman in a sarcastic manner: "Who's that guy in there playing my guitar!!!" (Because I didn't give anyone permission.) Norman looked up at me, then he looked through the double pane window into the musicians' room, and then he looked at me again and said, "That's Buddy Holly."

And he immediately punched the talk-back button into the other room and said, "Buddy, come in here and meet these guys from Raton." (Of course, I'd had an immediate attitude adjustment about him playing my guitar.) Buddy walked into the control room and Norman said, "Everybody, introduce yourselves to Buddy."

George Tomsco

Early in my recording career, my producer, Snuff Garrett, received a demo from the Holley family.
The song was called "Buddy's song." The writer was listed as Ella Holley (Buddy's mother), and the singer was Waylon Jennings (Buddy's friend, a KLLL disc jockey and musician).

The song was made up of Holly song titles loosely woven together to create a story line. It was a clever song, and I recorded it for my tribute album "I Remember Buddy Holly."

A year or so went by and, one day as I was listening to the song, I suddenly realized the melody sounded familiar. I dug out all of Buddy's records and apartment tapes and, sure enough, "Buddy's Song" shared the very same melody as "Peggy Sue Got Married"

Bobby Vee

When the group the Crickets broke up, it was the one and only time I ever saw Buddy cry.

Maria Elena Holly

It was years later, a friend of mine shared a tape he had found. It was my dad wishing Merry Christmas to his fans and I never heard my father wish me Merry Christmas.

Jay P. Richardson

'The Beatles' were originally called 'The Silver Beatles' and before that they were 'Johnny and The Moondogs'. They always played 'Think It Over' in the clubs.

Graham Nash

The original title of the song Chantilly Lace was You Know What I Like. The title of the song was changed for radio.

Jay P. Richardson

Not Fade Away was one of the first songs that I learned to play.

Geezer (Black Sabbath)

I was appearing with Elvis Presley and some others in Lubbock on April 10, 1956. I was 18 years old at the time. Buddy and the Crickets (actually Bob & Larry) opened the show. The local people all clearly loved him and his music, that's for sure.

Wanda Jackson

One of Buddy's favorite things to eat was tomato soup. His favorite architect was Frank Lloyd Wright. He had blueprints drawn up after he started making it big, for a house to be built for my grandparents. The house was never built. In the plans are a design for a recording studio and also one labeled "Buddy's room." In my opinion, he had plans on coming back often, or to even stay for a while, because he designed the studio and had a room specifically for himself.

Ingrid Kaiter

I was 18 years old. My sister called and told me the news. I refused to accept it as the truth until after the funeral
My own personal favorite memories of Buddy Holly was when we used to go out riding our motorcycles or going water skiing.

Joe B. Mauldin

I was celebrating my (17th) birthday on Feb. 2, which was the night of Buddy's last concert. Then when I found out that Buddy was dead, I remember I was standing on the corner on Langworthy Road in Salford, near Manchester (England). I was with my best friend, Allan Clarke, who later started the Hollies with me. We were distraught to say the least ... tears and more tears. We had lost a great friend ... one of us ... a rock star with glasses.

Graham Nash

We met Buddy at the Arnett-Benson Drug Store on College Avenue in Lubbock.

We were shocked and not able to believe what had happened. We had lost a close personal friend. We still miss him. His happy-go-lucky personality was contagious. He influenced our outlook and our appreciation of music.

Gary & Ramona Tollett

We never would see our mom cry, she was a very strong woman and we would only see her cry on February 3 and Ritchie's Birthday.

Connie Lemos

I want to thank all of Buddy's fans for keeping his music and memory alive; that consoles me.

Maria Elena Holly

When I learned of the 50th at the Surf I cleared my schedule to be here, to celebrate Buddy's music.

Graham Nash

Just listen to the lyrics of Buddy Holly. He was only twenty-two. Cole Porter would have been proud.

Sir Tim Rice

There was always music in our house. Our uncles would come over and sit Ritchie on their lap. They would show him how to hold the guitar, how to play the notes, and the chords. That's how he learned.

Connie Lemos

Lou Giordano called me and said 'Maria don't turn on the television'. Of course when someone tells you not to do something you do it. That's how I found out.

Maria Elena Holly

"Buddy Holly & The Crickets and my band, Ralna English and the Adlibs, were in a Battle of the Bands one Saturday night at a local movie theater in Lubbock. It was the Plaza Theater at 25th Street and Canton (Avenue), caddy corner from Roscoe Wilson School. Much to our surprise, Ralna English and the Adlibs beat Buddy Holly & The Crickets that night! I consider this my true "claim to fame." We had no idea at the time that Buddy would become the icon he has, and I am just honored to have known him."

Bob Burgess (The Adlibs)

I think there are a lot of people who don't realize what a talented singer Buddy was, not just a rock 'n' roller. Buddy and Bob Montgomery were performing at Hutchinson Jr. High when I was in the seventh grade, and I thought they were great then. Check out page 146 of the 1954 Lubbock High Westerner yearbook. Buddy was in the senior A choir, and he was a junior. Also on page 138: Bob won the round-up song contest with "Flower of My Heart."

Jerry "J.I." Allison

I was 20 years old when I was on my way out to the KLLL Radio transmitter, located at 50th Street and Quirt (now MLK) Avenue. Sky (Corbin, his brother) came on KLLL with the news and, for an hour or so, we thought Waylon (Jennings) also had been killed. The UPI (United Press International) wire story said it was Buddy and his band on the plane. One of the unfortunate things was that Sky was unaware that the Holleys had not been contacted, and we found out Mr. Holley first heard about Buddy's death on KLLL.
Sky and Slim (another brother) went to the Holleys' house the next day to explain and apologize. Everyone felt bad about running the UPI story, assuming they had been notified. But the Holleys learned about it on KLLL's news bulletin.

Larry Corbin

I spent the night at the Allison's folks' house. I was up the next morning visiting with J.I.'s mom when the lady who lived across the street came over and told us she had just heard it on the radio. J.I. and Peggy Sue were still asleep, and it became my sad task to wake them with the awful news.

Sonny Curtis

THE MUSIC THAT THESE THREE ENTERTAINERS GAVE US IS EMBEDDED DEEP INTO THE VERY CORE OF OUR EXISTENCE.

THEY ARE MORE THAN JUST POP ICONS OF OUR AMERICAN CULTURE. THEIR MUSIC SPEAKS TO OUR HEARTS AND AT SOME POINT HAS MADE US WHO WE ARE TODAY.

THEIR SONGS ARE MORE THAN JUST A BUNCH OF WORDS WITH CATCHY MELODIES, THEIR SONG HAVE A TIMELESS QUALITY THAT APPEAL TO EVERYONE (EVERYWHERE) AROUND THE WORLD

THEIR SONGS WILL CONTINUE TO BE HANDED DOWN FROM GENERATION TO GENERATION, THE SAME WAY A FAMILY MEMBER HANDS DOWN A PRECIOUS FAMILY HEIRLOOM.

CHARLES HARDIN HOLLEY/ RICHARD STEVEN VALENZUELA /JILES PERRY RICHARDSON AND ROGER ARTHUR PETERSON

THE MUSIC DIDNT DIE / THEY ARE IN OUR HEARTS / AND ON OUR MINDS (EVERYDAY)

Gary L Clevenger

TRIBUTE SONGS TO THE THREE STARS

AND BUDDY PLAYED PEGGY SUE
GOLD RECORDS IN THE SNOW
THE MAN I MET
THREE STARS
REAL BUDDY HOLLY STORY
TEENAGE HEAVEN
THREE YOUNG MEN
GOODNIGHT ROCK & ROLL
HEAVEN OF THE STARS
TRIBUTE TO BUDDY HOLLY
THE BUDDY I KNEW
HEY BUDDY
I NAMED MY LITTLE GIRL HOLLY
LOST WITHOUT YOU
NOW THAT YOU'RE GONE
OH BUDDY
AMERICAN PIE
WE REMEMBER RITCHIE VALENS
FOREVER 22
BUDDY HOLLY DAYS
TRIBUTE TO BUDDY HOLLY
MY BUDDY HOLLY DAYS
FORGET BUDDY HOLLY?
TRIBUTE TO THE LATE BUDDY HOLLY
I FEEL LIKE BUDDY HOLLY
I COULD HAVE BEEN BUDDY HOLLY
TRIBUTE TO BUDDY HOLLY
BUDDY BIG BOPPER RITCHIE
SKA VI ALSKA SA SKA VI ALSKA TILL BUDDY HOLLY
HELLO BUDDY
ROCK & ROLL IS BACK
BUDDY'S SONG
DO YOU REMEMBER BUDDY HOLLY
LEAVE IT IN THE HANDS OF FATE
THREE FRIENDS
BUDDYS GUITAR
THE STAGE
BUDDY HOLLY NOT FADE AWAY
NOW THAT YOURE GONE
LOOKIN' FOR THE HI-D-HO

SOME BOOKS AND OTHER PUBLICATIONS

BEHIND THE MUSIC - THE DAY THE MUSIC DIED SKINNER POCKET BOOKS 2000 PB NF
BEST OF BUDDY HOLLY MPL COMMUNICATIONS 1978 PB SONGBOOK
BUDDY HOLLY DAVE LAING ROCKBOOK 1971 PB NF
BUDDY HOLLY DAVE LAING COLLIER 1972 PB NF
BUDDY HOLLY TOM STOCKDALE PARRAGON 1995 HB NF
BUDDY HOLLY & CRICKETS ALBUM SOUTHERN MUSIC REPRINT OF 1958 PB SONGBOOK
BUDDY HOLLY & CRICKETS GREATEST HITS SOUTHERN MUSIC 1977 PB SONGBOOK BUDDY HOLLY & THE CRICKETS.
A. CLARKE PRIVATELY PUB. ND PB NF
BUDDY HOLLY A - Z ALAN MANN AURUM PRESS 1996 PB NF
BUDDY HOLLY A BIO IN WORDS E & R PEER. PEER INT'L 1972 PB NF
BUDDY HOLLY A COLLECTORS GUIDE
BUDDY HOLLY A TRIBUTE TO MAN/MUSIC TEXAS WIND 1983 PB NF
BUDDY HOLLY A-Z ALAN MANN PRIVATELY PUBLISHED 1994 PB NF
BUDDY HOLLY & THE CRICKETS MUSICAL HISTORY IN AUSTRALIA RODERICK JORDAN HANSEN PRINTERS 2007 PB NF
BUDDY HOLLY & THE CRICKETS MUSICAL HISTORY IN AUSTRALIA RODERICK JORDAN HANSEN PRINTERS 2008 HB NF
BUDDY HOLLY & THE CRICKETS THE UK TOUR JIM CARR HOLLY INTERNATIONAL PUBLISHING 2005 PB NF
BUDDY HOLLY BOOK FOR FANS ONLY
BUDDY HOLLY DAY-BY-DAY VOL 1 BILL GRIGGS PRIV. PUB. 1997 PB NF
BUDDY HOLLY DAY-BY-DAY VOL 2 BILL GRIGGS PRIV. PUB. 1997 PB NF
BUDDY HOLLY DAY-BY DAY VOL 3 BILL GRIGGS PRIV. PUB. 1997 PB NF
BUDDY HOLLY DAY-BY-DAY VOL 4 BILL GRIGGS PRIV. PUB. 1997 PB NF
BUDDY HOLLY DAY-BY-DAY VOL 5 BILL GRIGGS PRIV. PUB. 1997 PB NF
BUDDY HOLLY HIS LIFE & MUSIC JOHN GOLDROSEN CHARISMA 1975 NF
BUDDY HOLLY HIS LIFE & MUSIC JOHN GOLDROSEN PANTHER 1979 PB NF
BUDDY HOLLY HIS MUSIC MPL COMMUNICATIONS 1977 PB SONGBOOK
BUDDY HOLLY IS ALIVE & WELL ON GANYMEDE
BUDDY HOLLY LIVES WISE PUBLICATIONS 1978 PB SONGBOOK
BUDDY HOLLY NO 1 A CLARK NATIONAL ROCK/ROLL ARCHIVES 1989 PB
BUDDY HOLLY SOUVENIR ALBUM SOUTHERN MUSIC 1961 PB SONGBOOK
BUDDY HOLLY STORY MPL COMMUNICATIONS 1978 PB SONGBOOK
BUDDY HOLLY STORY COLUMBIA PICTURES PUB 1978 PB NF
BUDDY HOLLY STORY JOHN GOLDROSEN QUICK FOX 1979 PB NF
BUDDY HOLLY STORY JOHN TOBLER PLEXUS 1979 PB NF?
BUDDY HOLLY DAVE LAING MACMILLAN 1971 HB NF
BUDDY THE BIOGRAPHY PHILIP NORMAN PAN BOOKS 1997 HB NF
CHANTILLY LACE TIM KNIGHT PORT ARTHUR HIST SOC 1989 PB NF
DECK THE HALLS WITH BUDDY HOLLY GAVIN EDWARDS HARPER PERENNIAL 1998 PB HUMOR
ELVIS AND BUDDY ALAN MANN MUSIC MENTOR BOOKS 2002 PB NF
FALLING STARS RICH EVERITT HARBOR HOUSE 2004 HB NF

FLYING THE BEECH BONANZA JOHN ECKALBAR MCCORMICK-ARMSTRONG CO. 1986 HB NF
GOLDEN ANNIVERSARY SONGBOOK MPL COMMUNICATIONS 1986 PB SONGBOOK
I DON'T KNOW HOW I DID IT. LARRY HOLLEY PRIV. PUB. 2007 PB NF
LEGEND THAT IS BUDDY HOLLY
MUSIC'S BROKEN WINGS WM HEITMAN DREAMFLYER PUB. 2003 PB NF
RAVE ON PHILIP NORMAN SIMON & SCHUSTER 1996 PB NF
RAVE ON PHILIP NORMAN FIRESIDE/SIMON & SCHUSTER 1997 PB NF
REMEMBERING BUDDY (BUDDY HOLLY) JOHN GOLDROSEN & JOHN BEECHER PAVILION 1987 PB NF
REMEMBERING BUDDY (BUDDY HOLLY) JOHN GOLDROSEN & JOHN BEECHER DA CAPO PRESS 1996 PB NF
REMEMBERING BUDDY (BUDDY HOLLY) JOHN GOLDROSEN & JOHN BEECHER DA CAPO PRESS 1996 PB NF
RITCHIE VALENS A CLARK NATIONAL ROCK/ROLL ARCHIVES 1989 PB NF
RITCHIE VALENS FIRST LATINO ROCKER BEVERLY MENDHEIM BILINGUAL REVIEW PRESS 1987 PB NF
THOSE INCOMPARABLE BONANZAS
LARRY BALL MCCORMICK-ARMSTRONG 1989 HB NF
THE LAST TOUR   LARRY LEHMER
BUDDY HOLLY   ELLIS AMBURN
WHATEVER HAPPENED TO PEGGY SUE PEGGY SUE GERRON / GLENDA CAMERON 2008 TOGI HB NF

Credits:

Vicky and John Pickering / Don Larson / Bob Lee / Bob Hale / James McCool / Sevan Garabedian / Donna Burgess / Brandon Sinks / Sherry Holley / Scott Sriver / Sue Frederick / LHS Class of '55 / Jay P Richardson / Echo McGuire Griffith / Bill Griggs / Bob Lapham / George Tomsco / Andy Wilkinson / Tom and Peter Gibson / Clive Harvey / Tony Warran / Glenda Ward / John Beecher / Pete Carroll / Crickets File Magazine / Down The Line Magazine and The Crickets Sound Project.

And to every Buddy Holly, Ritchie Valens and Big Bopper fan around the world

THANK YOU

A special thank you to The Lubbock Avalanche journal – William Kerns and Terry Greenberg and to Doug Long for his friendship and generosity.

Front Cover Collage: Don Larson

Front Cover Layout: Scott Sriver / Back Cover Layout: Scott Sriver

Eau Claire Winter Dance Party Photos appear courtesy of Don Larson

Buddy Holly and The Crickets / Hershey Pennsylvania (58) photos appear courtesy of Bob Lee

Second Hand Bopper Memories appears courtesy of Jay P Richardson

Bob Hale photo appears courtesy of Bob Hale

John Pickering's Dream appears courtesy of Vicky and John Pickering

'Forever 22' and 'Buddy Holly Not Fade Away' appears courtesy of John Pickering Music

'Leave it in the Hands of Fate' appears courtesy of Andy Wilkinson

UK Edition edited and produced by Peter Gibson and Tony Warran.

Printed in Great
Britain
by Amazon